HINDU FASTS
AND FESTIVALS

HINDU FASTS
AND FESTIVALS

SRI SWAMI SIVANANDA

Published By

THE DIVINE LIFE SOCIETY
P.O. SHIVANANDANAGAR—249 192
Distt. Tehri-Garhwal, U.P., Himalayas, India

Price]   1993   [Rs. 25/-

Seventh Edition : 1993
(5,000 Copies)

ISBN 81-7052-039-8

Published by Swami Krishnananda for The Divine Life
Society, Shivanandanagar, and printed by him at the
Yoga-Vedanta Forest Academy Press, P.O. Shivananda-
nagar, Distt. Tehri-Garhwal, U.P., Himalayas, India

Publisher's Note

THE HINDUS are a profoundly religious people. Their goal of life is Self-realisation or the attainment of God-consciousness. A religion of some kind they must have—a religion which will stir the depths of the heart and give room for the exercise of faith, devotion and love.

All Hindu festivals have a deep spiritual import or high religious significance. All great Hindu festivals have religious, social and hygienic elements in them. In every festival there is bathing in the morning before sunrise in the river or tank or well. Every individual will have to do some Japa, prayer, Kirtan, recitation of Sanskrit verses and meditation.

Man gets tired on account of hard work or monotonous actions. He wants some change or variety. He wants relaxation. He wants something to cheer him up. These festivals make him cheerful and happy, and give him rest and peace.

In this book Gurudev has explained the significance and the philosophy of many of our fasts and festivals. In two aspects of these observances, he has always allowed the greatest freedom: (1) in the determination of the dates of the festival, which, as he has explained on page 53, vary, and (2) in the traditional ways of celebrating them. For instance, in South India during the Durga Puja they have the Kolu when various idols and toys are arranged in colourful gallaries before which, every evening, girls sit and sing. Again, in some places there is fire-walking without the Kavadi (see page 109), held in honour of Draupadi Amman who was born of fire; or in Ceylon, according to Yogi Satchidananda of Ceylon, in honour of Kannaki Amman. Gurudev never disturbs anyone's good beliefs and customs.

The way in which the most important festivals are observed at the Sivananda Ashram, Rishikesh, in India is also given in this volume. If we have no precedent, we can as well adopt that. On the particular day, it would be even enough to read the chapter relating to that day, to remind ourselves of the spirit of the occasion.

Gurudev observes in his Ashram not only the festivals of the Hindus but those of the Christians and the Muslims, too: an example for us to copy. In his eyes, there are no distinctions. The New Year's Day according to the English calendar has the same significance to him as the Tamil or the Telugu New Year's Day. Hence, when he talks of the Telugu New Year's Day in this book, it can well be read Tamil New Year's Day or Gujarati New Year's Day.

—*The Divine Life Society*

Contents

VRATAS (VOWS)

Prayers for All Occasions

Devotees and followers of Sri Gurudev Sivananda in South Africa and elsewhere, follow Gurudev's invariable custom of commencing all functions with the following invocatory Kirtans, and concluding them with the peace chants that follow.

INVOCATORY KIRTANS

Jaya Ganesha Jaya Ganesha Jaya Ganesha paahimaam
   Sri Ganesha Sri Ganesha Sri Ganesha rakshamaam
Jaya Saraswati Jaya Saraswati Jaya Saraswati paahimaam
   Sri Saraswati Sri Saraswati Sri Saraswati rakshamaam
Saravanabhava Saravanabhava Saravanabhava paahimaam
   Subramanya Subramanya Subramanya rakshamaam
Sivananda Sivananda Sivananda paahimaam
   Sivananda Sivananda Sivananda rakshamaam
Jaya Guru Shiva Guru Hari Guru Ram
   Jagad Guru Param Guru Sat Guru Shyam
Adi Guru Advaita Guru Ananda Guru Om
   Chit Guru Chitgana Guru Chinmaya Guru Om
Jaya Siya Ram Jaya Jaya Siya Ram (2)
Jaya Radhe Shyam Jaya Jaya Radhe Shyam (2)
Jaya Hanuman Jaya Jaya Hanuman (2)
Hare Rama Hare Rama Rama Rama Hare Hare, Hare
   Krishna Hare Krishna Krishna Krishna Hare Hare (3)
Sivananda Sivananda Sadguru Natha Sivananda.

MAHA MRITYUNJAYA MANTRA

Om trayambakam yajaamahe sugandhim pushtivardhanam
Urvaarukamiva bandhanaan mrityor muksheeya maamritaat.

CONCLUDING PEACE CHANTS

Sarveshaam swasti bhavatu, sarveshaam shaantir bhavatu,
Sarveshaam poornam bhavatu, sarveshaam mangalam bhavatu;
Sarve bhavantu sukhinah, sarve santu niraamayah,
Sarve bhadraani pashyantu, maakaschid duhkhabhaagbhavet;
  Asato maa sad gamaya
  Tamaso maa jyotir gamaya
  Mrityor maa amritam gamaya;
Om poornamadah poornamidam poornaatpoornamudachyate,
Poornasya poornamaadaaya poornamevaavashishyate.
    Om shaantih shaantih shaantih!

MEDITATION ON LORD SHIVA

Shaantam padmaasanastham shashadharamakutam
  panchavaktram trinetram,
Shoolam vajram cha khadgam parashumabhayadam
  dakshinaange vahantam;
Naagam paasham cha ghantaam damaruka sahitam
  chaankusham vaamabhaage,
Naanaalankaara deeptam sphatika maninibham
  paarvateesham namaami.

MEANING: I prostrate myself before the five-faced Lord of Parvati, who is adorned with various ornaments, who shines like the crystal jewel, who is seated peacefully in the lotus pose, with moon-crested crown, with three eyes, wearing trident, thunderbolt, sword and axe on the right side, who holds the serpent, noose, bell, *damaru* and spear on the left side, and who gives protection from all fear to His devotees.

MEDITATION ON SRI SHANKARACHARYA

*Padmaaseenam prashantam yamaniratamaanan
  gaari tulya prabhaavam,*
*Phaale bhasmaankitaam bhasmita rujira mukhaam
  bhojanindeevaraaksham;*
*Kambugreevam karaabhyaam avidtamurulasat
  pustakam jnaanamudraam,*
*Vandyam geervaana mukhyair natajana varadam
  bhaavaye shankaraaryam.*

MEANING: I meditate on Sri Shankaracharya who is seated in the lotus posture with Jnanamudra, who is calm, endowed with virtues like Yama, Niyama, etc., whose glory is as great as that of Lord Shiva, who wears the sacred ashes on the forehead, whose face resembles the blossomed lotus, with lotus-like eyes, possessing sacred books in hand, who is ever adored by people of high learning and wisdom, and who fulfils the desires of his devotees (who prostrate themselves before him).

MEDITATION ON LORD DATTATREYA

*Maalaakamandalu dharah karapadmayugme
  Madhyastha paaniyugale damarutrishoolam;*
*Adhyastha urdhva karayoh shubha shankhachakre
  Vande tamatrivaradam bhujashatkayuktam.*

MEANING: I meditate on Lord Dattatreya, the son of Atri, who has six hands, who holds the rosary and water-vessel in two hands, with *damaru* and spear in the other two hands, and with conch and discus in the upper two hands.

MEDITATION ON LORD GANESHA

Gajaananam bhootaganaadisevitam
  Kapittha jamboophala saara bhakshitam;
Umaasutam shoka vinaasha kaaranam
  Namaami vighneshwara paada pankajam.

MEANING: I worship the lotus feet of Ganesha, the son of Uma, the destroyer of all sorrows, who is served by the host of gods and elementals, and who takes the essence of the *kapittha-jambu* fruit (fruit resembling the *bilwa* fruit).

MEDITATION ON LORD SUBRAMANYA

Shadaananam kumkumaraktavarnam
  Mahaa matim divya mayoora vaahanam;
Rudrasya soonum sura sainyanaatham
  Guham sadaaham sharanam prapadye.

MEANING: I always take refuge in Lord Guha (Lord Subramanya) of six faces, who is of deep red colour and infinite knowledge, who has the divine peacock to ride on, the son of Lord Shiva and the leader of the army of the Devas.

Prayers for All Occasions

MEDITATION ON SRI KRISHNA

Vamshee vibhooshita karaan navaneeradaabhaat
Peetaambaraadaruna bimbaphalaa dharoshthaat;
Poornendusundara mukhaad aravinda netraat
Krishnaat param kimapi tattwam aham na jaane.

MEANING: I know not any other Reality than the lotus-eyed Krishna with hands adorned with flute, looking like a heavy-laden cloud in lustre, wearing a yellow silk garment, with His lower lip like a ruddy *bimba* fruit, and with face shining like the full moon.

MEDITATION ON SRI RAMA

Dhyaayedaajaanubaaham dhritasharadhanusham
  baddhapadmaasanastham,
Peetam vaaso vasaanam navakamala dala
  spardhinetram prasannam;
Vaamaankaaroodhaseetaa mukhakamala milal
  lochanam neeradaabham,
Naanaalankaara deeptam dadhatamuru jataa
  mandalam raamachandram.

MEANING: One should meditate on Sri Ramachandra, with hands reaching the knees, holding the bow and arrows, seated in the locked-up lotus posture, wearing a yellow garb, with eyes vying with the newly-blossomed lotus petals, with a pleasant gait, who has Sita seated on His left thigh, who is blue like the clouds, who is adorned with all kinds of ornaments and having a big circle of Jata on the head.

LORD VISHNU
His Mantra is: *Om Namo Narayanaya*
Suklambharadharam visnum sasi varnam caturbhujam
Prasanna vadanam dhyayet sarvavighnopasantaye

Chitra Purnima

THE TWELVE months of the Hindu year, based on the lunar calendar, are named after that star during whose ascendency the full moon of that month occurs. The full moon day of Chaitra month, that is, the Purnima during the ascendency of the Chitra star is particularly sacred to the Chitra Guptas, the recording angels of the Hindu pantheon. A special worship is offered to these celestial representatives of the god of death, and an offering of spiced rice is prepared and later distributed as *prasad* or holy sacrament. A fire worship is done at the close of the ritualistic worship. By the performance of this religious observance annually, these angels of the other world are greatly pleased and judge man's actions with more sympathy.

The psychological effect of this worship, done on the very first full moon day of every year (Chaitra is the first of the twelve months), is to vividly remind us of the higher power that maintains a constant watch over every act of ours on this earth-plane. This memory serves as an invisible check on one's conduct. The conception of the Chitra Guptas as located within each shoulder is a powerful inducement to keep oneself engaged in constantly doing good actions only.

The term Chitra Gupta means "hidden picture". A true picture of all our good and evil actions is preserved in the ethereal records. The Hindu personifies it for the sake of worship. The real significance of the worship of the Chitra Guptas is beautifully brought out in the following story connected with it.

Brihaspati is the Guru or preceptor of Indra, the king of the gods. Indra disobeyed Brihaspati on one occasion and the Guru relinquished his task of instructing Indra in what he should and should not do. During the period of the Guru's absence, Indra did many evil deeds. When the compassionate Guru resumed his duty again, Indra wanted to know what he should do to expiate the wrongs he had done in his Guru's absence. Brihaspati asked Indra to undertake a pilgrimage.

While Indra was on pilgrimage, he suddenly felt the load of sins taken off his shoulders at a certain place (near Madurai in South India), and he discovered a Shiva Lingam there. He attributed the miracle to this Lingam and wanted to build a temple for it. He had this constructed immediately. Now he wished to perform the worship of the Lingam; the Lord Himself caused golden lotuses to appear in a nearby pond. Indra was greatly pleased and blessed. The day on which he thus worshipped the Lord was Chitra Purnima.

When you perform worship on the Chitra Purnima day, remember this story. If you have intense faith, if

2

you feel with a contrite heart that you have committed sins on account of ignorance, if you pray with faith and devotion to the Lord to forgive your sins, if you resolve never to commit them in the future, and if you resolve to be obedient to your Guru and never to flout his counsel, then your sins will be forgiven. There is no doubt about this. This is the significance of the above story of Indra. Meditate on this story on Chitra Purnima day.

The Hindu scriptures prescribe elaborate worship of the Chitra Guptas on this day. The Deity is invoked in an image or a *kalasa* (vessel filled with water) and then worshipped with all the rituals and formalities of the worship offered to God's image. Meditate on Chitra Gupta, reciting the following verse:

Chitra guptam mahaa praajnam lekhaneepatra dhaarinam;
Chitra-ratnaambara-dhaaram madhyastham sarvadehinaam.

Then offer ritualistic worship with incense, camphor, flowers, etc. Feed some Brahmins, the poor and the needy. Give bountifully in charity and receive the Lord's blessings.

Deepavali

DEEPAVALI or Diwali means "a row of lights". It falls on the last two days of the dark half of Kartik (October-November). For some it is a three-day festival. It commences with the Dhan-Teras, on the 13th day of the dark half of Kartik, followed the next day by the Narak Chaudas, the 14th day, and by Deepavali proper on the 15th day.

There are various alleged origins attributed to this festival. Some hold that they celebrate the marriage of Lakshmi with Lord Vishnu. In Bengal the festival is dedicated to the worship of Kali. It also commemorates that blessed day on which the triumphant Lord Rama returned to Ayodhya after defeating Ravana. On this day also Sri Krishna killed the demon Narakasura.

In South India people take an oil bath in the morning and wear new clothes. They partake of sweetmeats. They light fireworks which are regarded as the effigies of Narakasura who was killed on this day. They greet one another, asking, "Have you had your Ganges bath?" which actually refers to the oil bath that morning as it is regarded as purifying as a bath in the holy Ganges.

Everyone forgets and forgives the wrongs done by others. There is an air of freedom, festivity and friendliness everywhere. This festival brings about unity. It instils charity in the hearts of people. Everyone buys new clothes for the family. Employers, too, purchase new clothes for their employees.

Waking up during the Brahmamuhurta (at 4a.m.) is a great blessing from the standpoint of health, ethical discipline, efficiency in work and spiritual advancement. It is on Deepavali that everyone wakes up early in the morning. The sages who instituted this custom must have cherished the hope that their descendents would realise its benefits and make it a regular habit in their lives.

In a happy mood of great rejoicing village folk move about freely, mixing with one another without any reserve, all enmity being forgotten. People embrace one another with love. Deepavali is a great unifying force. Those with keen inner spiritual ears will clearly hear the voice of the sages, "O Children of God! unite, and love all". The vibrations produced by the greetings of love which fill the atmosphere are powerful enough to bring about a change of heart in every man and woman in the world. Alas! That heart has considerably hardened, and only a continuous celebration of Deepavali in our homes can rekindle in us the urgent need of turning away from the ruinous path of hatred.

On this day Hindu merchants in North India open their new account books and pray for success and prosperity during the coming year. The homes are cleaned and decorated by day and illuminated by night with earthern oil-lamps. The best and finest illuminations are to be seen in Bombay and Amritsar. The famous Golden Temple at Amritsar is lit in the evening with thousands of lamps placed all over the steps of the big tank. Vaishnavites celebrate the Govardhan Puja and feed the poor on a large scale.

O Ram! The light of lights, the self-luminous inner light of the Self is ever shining steadily in the chamber of your heart. Sit quietly. Close your eyes. Withdraw the senses. Fix the mind on this supreme light and enjoy the real Deepavali, by attaining illumination of the soul.

He who Himself sees all but whom no one beholds, who illumines the intellect, the sun, the moon and the stars and the whole universe but whom they cannot illumine, He indeed is Brahman, He is the inner Self. Celebrate the real Deepavali by living in Brahman, and enjoy the eternal bliss of the soul.

The sun does not shine there, nor do the moon and the stars, nor do lightnings shine and much less fire. All the lights of the world cannot be compared even to a ray of the inner light of the Self. Merge yourself in this light of lights and enjoy the supreme Deepavali.

Many Deepavali festivals have come and gone. Yet the hearts of the vast majority are as dark as the night of the new moon. The house is lit with lamps, but the heart is full of the darkness of ignorance. O man! wake up from the slumber of ignorance. Realise the constant and eternal light of the Soul which neither rises nor sets, through meditation and deep enquiry.

Deepavali

May you all attain full inner illumination! May the supreme light of lights enlighten your understanding! May you all attain the inexhaustible spiritual wealth of the Self! May you all prosper gloriously on the material as well as spiritual planes!

3

Durga Puja or Navaratri

SALUTATIONS to the Divine Mother, Durga, who exists in all beings in the form of intelligence, mercy, beauty, who is the consort of Lord Shiva, who creates, sustains and destroys the universe.

This festival is observed twice a year, once in the month of Chaitra and then in Aswayuja. It lasts for nine days in honour of the nine manifestations of Durga. During Navaratri (the word literally means "nine nights") devotees of Durga observe a fast. Brahmins are fed and prayers are offered for the protection of health and property.

The beginning of summer and the beginning of winter are two very important junctions of climatic and solar influence. These two periods are taken as sacred opportunities for the worship of the Divine Mother. They are indicated respectively by the Rama-Navaratri in Chaitra (April-May) and the Durga Navaratri in Aswayuja (September-October). The bodies and minds of people undergo a considerable change on account of the changes in Nature. Sri Rama is worshipped during Ramnavmi, and Mother Durga during Navaratri.

Durga Puja or Navaratri

The Durga Puja is celebrated in various parts of India in different styles. But the one basic aim of this celebration is to propitiate Shakti, the Goddess in Her aspect as Power, to bestow upon man all wealth, auspiciousness, prosperity, knowledge (both sacred and secular), and all other potent powers. Whatever be the particular or special request that everyone may put before the Goddess, whatever boon may be asked of Her, the one thing behind all these is propitiation, worship and linking oneself with Her. There is no other aim. This is being effected consciously or unconsciously. Everyone is blessed with Her loving mercy and is protected by Her.

Durga Puja or Navaratri commences on the first and ends on the tenth day of the bright half of Aswayuja (September-October). It is held in commemoration of the victory of Durga over Mahishasura, the buffalo-headed demon. In Bengal Her image is worshipped for nine days and then cast into water. The tenth day is called Vijaya Dasami or Dussera (the "tenth day"). Processions with Her image are taken out along the streets of villages and cities.

The mother of Durga (that is, the wife of the King of the Himalayas) longed to see her daughter. Durga was permitted by Lord Shiva to visit her beloved mother only for nine days in the year. The festival of Durga Puja marks this brief visit and ends with the Vijaya Dasami day, when Goddess Durga leaves for Her return to Mount Kailas. This is the view of some devotees.

9

In Bengal, Durga Puja is a great festival. All who live away from home return during the Puja days. Mothers reunite with their sons and daughters, and wives with their husbands.

The potter shows his skill in making images, the painter in drawing pictures, the songster in playing on his instrument, and the priest in reciting the sacred books. The Bengalis save money throughout the year only to spend everything during the Puja days. Cloth is freely distributed to the Brahmins.

The woman of Bengal welcomes the Goddess with a mother's love and sends away the image on the last day, with every ceremony associated with a daughter's departure to her husband's home and with motherly tears in her eyes. This signifies the parting of Durga from Her beloved mother.

Durga Puja is the greatest Hindu festival in which God is adored as Mother. Hinduism is the only religion in the world which has emphasised to such an extent the motherhood of God. One's relationship with one's mother is the dearest and the sweetest of all human relations. Hence, it is proper to look upon God as mother.

Durga represents the Divine Mother. She is the energy aspect of the Lord. Without Durga, Shiva has no expression and without Shiva, Durga has no existence. Shiva is the soul of Durga; Durga is identical with Shiva. Lord Shiva is only the silent witness. He is motionless, absolutely changeless. He is not affected by the cosmic play. It is Durga who does everything.

Shakti is the omnipotent power of the Lord, or the Cosmic Energy. The Divine Mother is represented as having ten different weapons in Her hands. She sits on a lion. She keeps up the play of the Lord through the three attributes of Nature, namely, Sattwa, Rajas and Tamas. Knowledge, peace, lust, anger, greed, egoism and pride, are all Her forms.

You will find in the Devi Sukta of the *Rig Veda Samhita* that Vak, symbolising speech, the daughter of the sage Anbhirna, realised her identity with the Divine Mother, the Power of the Supreme Lord, which manifests throughout the universe among the gods, among men and beasts and among the creatures of the deep ocean.

In the *Kena Upanishad*, you will find that the Divine Mother shed wisdom on Indra and the gods and said that the gods were able to defeat the demons only with the help of the power of the Supreme Lord.

The worship of Devi, the universal Mother, leads to the attainment of knowledge of the Self. The story in the *Kena Upanishad* known as the "Yaksha Prasna", supports this view. It tells how Uma, the Divine Mother, taught the Truth to the gods. Goddess Shakti thus sheds wisdom on Her devotees.

Devi worship is, therefore, worship of God's glory, of God's greatness and supremacy. It is adoration of the Almighty. It is unfortunate that Devi is ignorantly understood by many as a mere blood-thirsty Hindu Goddess. No! Devi is not a vicious demoness nor is She the property of the Hindus alone. Devi does not belong to any religion. Devi is that conscious power of God. The words Devi, Shakti, etc., and the ideas of different forms connected with these names are concessions granted by the sages due to the limitations of the human intellect; they are by no means the ultimate definitions of Shakti.

The original or Adi Shakti is beyond human comprehension. Bhagavan Krishna says in the *Gita*: "This is only My lower nature. Beyond this is My higher nature, the life-principle which sustains the universe".

The *Upanishad* also says: "The supreme power of God is manifested in various ways. This power is of the nature of God, manifesting as knowledge, strength and activity".

Truly speaking, all beings in the universe are Shakti-worshippers, whether they are aware of it or not, for there is no one who does not love and long for power in some form or other. Physicists and scientists have now proved that everything is pure, imperishable energy. This energy is only a form of divine Shakti which exists in every form.

A child is more familiar with the mother than with the father, because the mother is very kind, loving, tender and affectionate and looks after the needs of the child. In the spiritual field also, the aspirant or the devotee—the spiritual child—has an intimate relationship with the Mother Durga, more than with the Father Shiva. Therefore, it behoves the aspirant to approach the Mother first, who then introduces Her spiritual child to the Father for his illumination.

MOTHER DURGA
The Saviour from all Sorrows and Dangers

13

The Mother's Grace is boundless. Her mercy is illimitable; Her knowledge infinite; Her power immeasurable; Her glory ineffable; and Her splendour indescribable. She gives you material prosperity as well as spiritual freedom.

Approach Her with an open heart. Lay bare your heart to Her with frankness and humility. Be as simple as a child. Kill ruthlessly the enemies of egoism, cunningness, selfishness and crookedness. Make a total, unreserved, and ungrudging self-surrender to Her. Sing Her praise. Repeat Her Name. Worship Her with faith and unflinching devotion. Perform special worship on the Navaratri days. Navaratri is the most suitable occasion for doing intense spiritual practices. These nine days are very sacred to the Divine Mother. Plunge yourself in Her worship. Practise intense repetition of the Divine Name, having a regular "quota" of repetitions per day, and the number of hours spent on it.

Devi fought with Bhandasura and his forces for nine days and nine nights. This Bhandasura had a wonderful birth and life. When Lord Shiva burnt Cupid with the fire of His "third eye", Sri Ganesha playfully moulded a figure out of the ashes, and the Lord breathed life into it! This was the terrible demon Bhandasura. He engaged himself in great penance and on account of it obtained a boon from Lord Shiva. With the help of that boon, he began harassing the worlds. The Divine Mother fought with him for nine nights (the demons have extraordinary strength during the night), and killed him on the evening of the tenth day, known as the Vijaya Dasami. The learning of any science is begun on this highly auspicious day. It was on this day that Arjuna worshipped Devi, before starting the battle against the Kauravas on the field of Kurukshetra.

Sri Rama worshipped Durga at the time of the fight with Ravana, to invoke Her aid in the war. This was on the days preceding the Vijaya Dasami day. He fought and won through Her Grace.

In days of yore, kings used to undertake ambitious expeditions on the day of the Vijaya Dasami. Those kings who did not go on such expeditions used to go out hunting in the deep forests. In Rajputana, India, even up to this date, people arrange mock attacks on some fort on Vijaya Dasami.

This day, however, has much to do with the life of Sri Rama. Nowhere in the history of the world can we find a parallel to the character of Sri Rama as a man, son, brother, husband, father or king. Maharishi Valmiki has exhausted the entire language in describing the glory of Sri Rama. And, we shall be rightly celebrating the Dussera if we make honest efforts to destroy the demon of our ego, and radiate peace and love wherever we go. Let us all resolve to become men of sterling character. Let us resolve and act. The story of Sri Rama is known in almost all parts of the globe, and if we but succeed in following even a hundredth part of His teachings, we shall make our lives more fragrant than the rose and more lustrous than gold!

Dussera can also be interpreted as "Dasa-Hara",

which means the cutting of the ten heads of Ravana. So, let us resolve today to cut the ten heads—passion, pride, anger, greed, infatuation, lust, hatred, jealousy, selfishness and crookedness—of the demon, Ego, and thus justify the celebration of Dussera.

Religious observances, traditional worship and observances at times have more than one significance. Apart from being the adoration of the Divine, they commemorate stirring events in history, they are allegoric when interpreted from the occult standpoint and, lastly, they are deeply significant pointers and revealing guides to the individual on his path to God-realisation.

Outwardly, the nine-day worship of Devi is a celebration of triumph. This nine days' celebration is offered to the Mother for Her successful struggle with the formidable demons led by Mahishasura. But, to the sincere spiritual aspirant, the particular division of the Navaratri into sets of three days to adore different aspects of the Supreme Goddess has a very sublime, yet thoroughly practical truth to reveal. In its cosmic aspect, it epitomises the stages of the evolution of man into God, from Jivahood (the state of individualisation) to Shivahood (the state of Self-realisation). In its individual import, it shows the course that his spiritual practice should take.

Let us, therefore, examine in detail the spiritual significance of Navaratri.

The central purpose of existence is to recognise your eternal identity with the supreme Spirit. It is to grow

MOTHER KALI
The Destroyer of Demoniac Attributes

17

into the image of the Divine. The supreme One embodies the highest perfection. It is spotless purity. To recognise your identity with That, to attain union with That, is verily to grow into the very likeness of the Divine. The aspirant, therefore, as his initial step, has to get rid of all the countless impurities, and the demoniacal elements that have come to cling to him in his embodied state. Then he has to acquire lofty virtues and auspicious, divine qualities. Thus purified, knowledge flashes upon him like the brilliant rays of the sun upon the crystal waters of a perfectly calm lake.

This process demands a resolute will, determined effort, and arduous struggle. In other words, strength and infinite power are the prime necessity. Thus it is the Divine Mother who has to operate through the aspirant.

Let us now consider how, on the first three days, the Mother is adored as supreme power and force, as Durga the Terrible. You pray to Mother Durga to destroy all your impurities, your vices, your defects. She is to fight with and annihilate the baser animal qualities in the spiritual aspirant, the lower, diabolical nature in him. Also, She is the power that protects your spiritual practice from its many dangers and pitfalls. Thus the first three days, which mark the first stage or the destruction of impurity and determined effort and struggle to root out the evil tendencies in your mind, are set apart for the worship of the destructive aspect of the Mother.

Once you have accomplished your task on the

negative side, that of breaking down the impure propensities and old vicious habits, the next step is to build up a sublime spiritual personality, to acquire positive qualities in place of the eliminated demoniacal qualities. The divine qualities that Lord Krishna enumerates in the *Gita*, have to be acquired. The aspirant must cultivate and develop all the auspicious qualities. He has to earn immense spiritual wealth to enable him to pay the price for the rare gem of divine wisdom. If this development of the opposite qualities is not undertaken in right earnest, the old demoniacal nature will raise its head again and again. Hence, this stage is as important in an aspirant's career as the previous one. The essential difference is: the former is a ruthless, determined annihilation of the filthy egoistic lower self; the latter is an orderly, steady, calm and serene effort to develop purity. This pleasanter side of the aspirant's Sadhana is depicted by the worship of Mother Lakshmi. She bestows on Her devotees the inexhaustible divine wealth or Deivi Sampath. Lakshmi is the wealth-giving aspect of God. She is purity itself. Thus the worship of Goddess Lakshmi is performed during the second set of three days.

Once the aspirant succeeds in routing out the evil propensities, and develops Sattwic or pure, divine qualities, he becomes competent to attain wisdom. He is now ready to receive the light of supreme wisdom. He is fit to receive divine knowledge. At this stage comes the devout worship of Mother Saraswathi, who is divine knowledge personified, the embodiment of knowledge of the Absolute. The sound of Her celestial *veena* awakens the notes of the sublime utterances of the *Upanishads* which reveal the Truth, and the sacred monosyllable, Om. She bestows the knowledge of the supreme, mystic sound and then gives full knowledge of the Self as represented by Her pure, dazzling snow-white apparel. Therefore, to propitiate Saraswathi, the giver of knowledge, is the third stage.

The tenth day, Vijaya Dasami, marks the triumphant ovation of the soul at having attained liberation while living in this world, through the descent of knowledge by the Grace of Goddess Saraswathi. The soul rests in his own Supreme Self or Satchidananda Brahman. This day celebrates the victory, the achievement of the goal. The banner of victory flies aloft. Lo! I am He! I am He!

This arrangement also has a special significance in the aspirant's spiritual evolution. It marks the indispensable stages of evolution through which everyone has to pass. One naturally leads to the other; to short-circuit this would inevitably result in a miserable failure. Nowadays many ignorant seekers aim straight at the cultivation of knowledge without the preliminaries of purification and acquisition of the divine qualities. They then complain that they are not progressing on the path. How can they? Knowledge will not descend until the impurities have been washed out, and purity is developed. How can the pure plant grow in impure soil?

Therefore adhere to this arrangement; your efforts will be crowned with sure success. This is your path. As you destroy one evil quality, develop the virtue opposite

MOTHER SARASWATHI
The presiding Deity over Creation and Dissolution

21

to it. By this process you will soon bring yourself up to that perfection which will culminate in identity with the Self which is your goal. Then all knowledge will be yours: you will be omniscient, omnipotent and you will feel your omnipresence. You will see your Self in all. You will have achieved eternal victory over the wheel of births and deaths, over the demon of worldliness. No more pain, no more misery, no more birth, no more death! Victory, victory be yours!

Glory to the Divine Mother! Let Her take you, step by step to the top of the spiritual ladder and unite you with the Lord!

At the Sivananda Ashram, Rishikesh, the following are the regular features during the Durga Puja celebrations:

1. A special ritualistic worship of the Mother is conducted daily, which includes the recitation of the *Durga Saptashati*.

2. Laksharchana for the Mother in the temple, with recitation of the *Sri Lalita Sahasranama*, is also conducted.

3. All are exhorted to do the maximum number of Japa of the Navarna Mantra, *Aim hreem kleem chaamundaayai vichche*, or the Mantra of their own tutelary Deity.

4. An elaborately decorated altar is set up for the evening Satsangs, with the picture of Mother Durga for the first three days, Mother Lakshmi for the next three days, and Mother Saraswathi for the last three days. Many sacred verses from the scriptures are recited and

many Kirtans are sung. The *Durga Saptashati* or the *Devi Mahatmya* is recited and explained in discourses. The function concludes with the formal floral worship and Arati. Sometimes scenes from the *Devi Mahatmya* are also enacted.

5. Earnest spiritual aspirants fast with milk and fruits only on all the nine days, or at least once in each of the three three-day periods.

6. Besides the books representing Saraswathi, all instruments and implements like typewriters, printing machinery, etc., are also worshipped on the ninth day.

7. On the Vijaya Dasami day, all aspirants *en masse* are given initiation into various Mantras according to their tutelary Deities. Deserving aspirants are initiated into the holy order of Sannyas. Initiation in the study of the alphabets is given to young children, and to the old children also! New students commence their lessons in music, etc. During the morning Satsang the books which were worshipped on the ninth day are again worshipped and a chapter from each of the principal scriptures like the *Gita, Upanishads, Brahma Sutras, Ramayana,* and *Srimad Bhagavatam* is recited.

8. On the Vijaya Dasami day, there is Kanya Puja also. Nine girls below the age of ten are worshipped as the embodiment of the Divine Mother. They are fed sumptuously and, amongst other things, presented with new clothes.

9. On this last day a grand *havan* is conducted in the temple, with recitation of the *Durga Saptashati* and other verses in praise of the Divine Mother.

4

Gayatri Japa Day

TO BRING to one's mind repeatedly the inspiring lives of great personalities, the wise men of all the ancient religions had set apart particular days in the year, as specially sacred and auspicious on their account. On these days, nations and races glorify these lofty personalities, they re-live the spirit of the great events to perpetuate the memory of these great men. Thus we find that the calendar of the Hindus is marked by birthdays of divine incarnations, saints and sages, the Gita Jayanthi, Guru Purnima, Shivaratri, Vaikunta Ekadashi, and many more auspicious occasions. The Gayatri Japa Day is one such very holy and glorious day intended to remind all of the greatest and most glorious of all Mantras, the sacred Gayatri Mantra.

The Gayatri is the life and support of every true Hindu. It is the impregnable spiritual armour, the veritable fortress, that guards and protects its votary. In fact, that is the very meaning of the word Gayatri— "that which protects one who sings it".

The Gayatri is the divine power that transforms the human into the Divine and blesses man with the

24

brilliant light of the highest spiritual illumination. Whoever may be one's favourite Deity, the regular repetition of a few *malas* (rosary of a hundred and eight beads) of Gayatri Japa every day will shower upon one incalculable benefits and blessings. It is universally applicable, being purely an earnest prayer for light addressed to the Almighty Supreme Spirit. The Para Brahma Gayatri Mantra is the most important of all Mantras. For every Brahmin of any creed or order of life, this has been prescribed as being the sole transcendental guiding light. The Brahmachari or celibate, the Grihastha or householder, and the Vanaprastha or one who is retired, must repeat this Mantra every day; the Sannyasin or renunciate is asked to repeat Om instead of this Mantra.

The nature of the Gayatri Mantra is such that you can repeat it while meditating on any form you like. It is generally conceived of as a female Deity by the majority of devotees. One who worships God as Mother adheres to this belief. But, in its true light, the Gayatri never speaks of a female at all. You cannot find a single word in the entire Gayatri Mantra, which speaks of a female. The feminine form of the word "Gayatri" cannot make its Deity a female. It is only the name of its metre and not the Deity.

Some people think that the Gayatri Mantra is presided over by the sun. In fact, even this idea is to be modified a little. The sun that it speaks of is not that which shines over this earth before our physical eyes, but *tat savituh* or "that Sun", the great Sun which this sun or moon does not illumine, and which is the impersonal, absolute Brahman.

Therefore, this is the greatest of all Mantras as its presiding Deity is none other than Para Brahman Himself. Hence, why hanker after other Mantras? The Gayatri itself is the crest-jewel or the king of all Mantras. It is the most powerful of all Mantras. *Na gayatryah paro mantrah*—"There is no Mantra greater than the Gayatri".

Each word, each letter of the Gayatri bears on its head the highest Vedantic concept of the absolute, supreme Truth. Do Japa of the Gayatri—it will give you the most excellent fruit, the fruit of immortality! The Mantra is as follows:

Om bhur bhuvah svah
Tat savitur varenyam
Bhargo devasya dheemahi
Dhiyo yo nah prachodayaat.

Om: symbol of Para Brahman.
Bhuh: Bhu Loka or the physical plane.
Bhuvah: the astral plane.
Svah: the celestial plane.
Tat: That; the transcendental Paramatma; God.
Savituh: the Creator.
Varenyam: fit to be worshipped.
Bhargah: remover of sins and ignorance; glory, effulgence.
Devasya: resplendent, shining.

26

Dheemahi: we meditate.
Dhiyah: the intellect, understanding.
Yo: who.
Nah: our.
Prachodayaat: enlighten, guide, impel.

MEANING: "We meditate on the glory of the Creator who has created the universe, who is fit to be worshipped, who is the embodiment of knowledge and light, who is the remover of all sins and ignorance. May He enlighten our intellect!"

Herein there are five parts: *Om* is the first part; *Bhur bhuvah svah* is the second; *Tat savitur varenyam* is the third; *Bhargo devasya dheemahi* is the fourth; and *Dhiyo yo nah prachodayaat* is the last. While chanting the Mantra you should pause after every part.

This rare and most precious divine treasure of the Gayatri Mantra is neglected by the youth of the present day. This is a very serious lapse indeed. Open your eyes now on this sacred day and start in right earnest the Japa of the Gayatri. Repeat it at least 108 times (1,008 is better!) on the Gayatri Japa day. Then continue it (at least 108 times daily) without missing even a single day.

May the whole world be made Gayatri-conscious through the inspiration of the auspicious Gayatri Japa Day! May you all be thrice blessed by taking the vow of daily Gayatri Japa right from this very moment! May you realise the inner Truth of the Gayatri Mantra!

Gayatri Japa is observed on the day after the Raksha Bandhan or Avani Avittam (July-August).

5

Guru Purnima

THE FULL moon day in the month of Ashad (July-August) is an extremely auspicious and holy day of Guru Purnima. On this day, sacred to the memory of the great sage, Bhagavan Sri Vyasa, Sannyasins settle at some place to study and discourse on the thrice-blessed *Brahma Sutras* composed by Maharishi Vyasa, and engage themselves in Vedantic, philosophical investigation.

Sri Vyasa has done unforgettable service to humanity for all times by editing the four *Vedas*, writing the eighteen *Puranas*, the *Mahabharata* and the *Srimad Bhagavata*. We can only repay the deep debt of gratitude we owe him, by constant study of his works and practice of his teachings imparted for the regeneration of humanity in this iron age. In honour of this divine personage, all spiritual aspirants and devotees perform Vyasa Puja on this day, and disciples worship their spiritual preceptor. Saints, monks and men of God are honoured and entertained with acts of charity by all the householders with deep faith and sincerity. The period Chaturmas (the "four months") begins from this day; Sannyasins stay at one place during the ensuing four rainy months, engaging in the study of the *Brahma Sutras* and the practice of meditation.

Mark fully the deep significance of this great day. It heralds the setting in of the eagerly awaited rains. The water drawn up and stored as clouds in the hot summer now manifests in plentiful showers that usher in the advent of fresh life everywhere. Even so, all begin seriously to put into actual practice all the theory and philosophy that have been stored up in them through patient study. Aspirants commence or resolve to intensify with all earnestness, their practical spiritual Sadhana right from this day.

Generate fresh waves of spirituality. Let all that you have read, heard, seen and learnt become transformed, through Sadhana, into a continuous outpouring of universal love, ceaseless loving service, and continuous prayer and worship of the Lord seated in all beings.

Live on milk and fruit on this day and practise rigorous Japa and meditation. Study the *Brahma Sutras* and do Japa of your Guru Mantra, during the four months following the Guru Purnima. You will be highly benefited.

The day of worship of one's preceptor, is a day of pure joy to the sincere spiritual aspirant. Thrilled by the expectation of offering his reverent homage to the beloved Guru, aspirants await this occasion with eagerness and devotion. It is the Guru alone that breaks the binding cords of attachment and releases the aspirant from the trammels of earthly existence.

The *Srutis* say: "To that high-souled aspirant, whose devotion to the Lord is great and whose devotion to his Guru is as great as that to the Lord, the secrets explained herein become illuminated". Guru is Brahman, the Absolute, or God Himself. He guides and inspires you from the innermost core of your being. He is everywhere.

Have a new angle of vision. Behold the entire universe as the form of the Guru. See the guiding hand, the awakening voice, the illuminating touch of the Guru in every object in this creation. The whole world will now stand transformed before your changed vision. The world as Guru will reveal all the precious secrets of life to you, and bestow wisdom upon you. The supreme Guru, as manifested in visible nature, will teach you the most valuable lessons of life.

Worship daily this Guru of Gurus, the Guru who taught even the Avadhuta Dattatreya. Dattatreya, regarded as God and the Guru of Gurus, considered Nature Herself as His Guru, and learnt a number of lessons from Her twenty-four creatures, and hence he is said to have had twenty-four Gurus. The silent, all-enduring earth with its lofty forbearance, the shady fruit-bearing tree with its willing self-sacrifice, the mighty banyan tree reposing with patience in the tiny seed, the drops of rain whose persistence wears away even the rocks, the planets and the seasons with their orderly punctuality and regularity were all divine Gurus to him. They who will look and listen, will learn.

Become a personification of receptivity. Empty

yourself of your petty ego. All the treasures locked up in the bosom of Nature will become yours. You will progress and attain perfection in an amazingly short time. Become pure and unattached as the mountain breeze. As the river flows continuously, steadily and constantly towards its goal, the ocean, so also let your life flow ceaselessly towards the supreme state of absolute Existence-Knowledge-Bliss, by letting all your thoughts, all your words and all your actions be directed only towards the goal.

The moon shines by reflecting the dazzling light of the sun. It is the full moon on the Purnima day that reflects in full splendour the glorious light of the sun. It glorifies the sun. Purify yourself through the fire of selfless service and Sadhana, and like the full moon, reflect the glorious light of the Self. Become the full reflectors of Brahmic splendour, the light of lights. Make this your goal: "I will be a living witness to divinity, the brilliant Sun of suns!"

The Supreme Self alone is real. He is the Soul of all. He is all-in-all. He is the essence of this universe. He is the unity that never admits of a duality under all the varieties and diversities of nature. Thou art this immortal, all-pervading, all-blissful Self. Thou art That! Realise this and be free.

Remember these four important lines of the *Brahma Sutras*:

1. *Athatho brahma jijnasaa*—Now, therefore, the enquiry of Brahman

2. *Janmasya yathah*—From which proceed the origin, etc.

3. *Sastra yonitwat*—The scriptures are the means of right knowledge.

4. *Tat tu samanvayat*—For, That is the main support (of the universe).

Jaya Guru Shiva Guru Hari Guru Ram;
Jagad Guru Param Guru Sat Guru Shyam.

It is through the medium of the preceptor that the individual can raise himself to Cosmic Consciousness. It is through that medium that the imperfect can become perfect, the finite can become infinite and the mortal can pass into the eternal life of blessedness. The Guru is verily a link between the individual and the Immortal. He is a being who has raised himself from *this* to *That* and thus has a free and unhampered access to both realms. He stands, as it were, upon the threshold of immortality, and, bending down, he raises the struggling individuals with his one hand, and with the other, lifts them up into the kingdom of everlasting joy and infinite Truth-Consciousness.

Do you realise now the sacred significance and the supreme importance of the Guru's role in the evolution of man? It was not without reason that the India of the past carefully tended and kept alive the lamp of Guru-Tattva. It is therefore not without reason that India, year after year, age after age, commemorates anew this ancient concept of the Guru, adores it and pays homage to it again and again, and thereby re-affirms its belief and allegiance to it. For, the true Indian knows that the Guru is the only guarantee for the individual to transcend the bondage of sorrow and death, and experience the Consciousness of the Reality.

Give up the delusive notion that to submit to the preceptor, to obey him and to carry out his instructions, is slavish mentality. Only the ignorant man thinks that it is beneath his dignity and against his freedom to submit to another man's command. This is a grave blunder. If you reflect carefully, you will see that your individual freedom is in reality an absolute abject slavery to your own ego and vanity. It is the vagary of the sensual mind. He who attains victory over the mind and the ego is the truly free man. He is the hero. It is to attain this victory that a man submits to the higher, spiritualised personality of the Guru. By this submission he vanquishes his lower ego and realises the bliss and freedom of the infinite Consciousness.

To strengthen and affirm the faith of the wavering man and to guarantee the attitude that is necessary for the fruition of all worship, the ancients have deified the personality of the Guru. To adore the Guru is indeed to adore the Supreme. In this world of mortality, the Guru is verily like an ambassador in an alien court. Just as an ambassador represents fully the nation to which he belongs, even so, the Guru is one who is the representative of the sublime transcendental state which he has attained. Just as to honour the ambassador is to honour the nation that he hails from, even so to worship and to offer adoration to the visible Guru is verily the direct worship and adoration of the Supreme Reality. Even as a distant tree though it cannot be seen is nevertheless known by the fragrance its fully-bloomed flowers waft far and wide, so also, the Guru is the divine flower who disseminates the Atmic aroma of divinity in this world, and thus proclaims the immortal Lord who is invisible to the physical eye. He is the standing witness to the Supreme Self, the counterpart of the Lord on earth, and through worship of him one attains the Self.

Remember and adore Sri Vyasa and the Gurus who are fully established in knowledge of the Self. May their blessings be upon you! May you cut asunder the knot of ignorance and shine as blessed sages shedding peace, joy and light everywhere!

At the Sivananda Ashram, Rishikesh, the Guru Purnima is celebrated every year on a grand scale. Many devotees and aspirants come from all parts of the country.

1. All aspirants awake at Brahmamuhurta, at 4 o'clock. They meditate on the Guru and chant his prayers.

2. Later in the day, the sacred worship of the Guru's Feet is performed. Of this worship it is said in the *Guru Gita*:

Dhyaana moolam guror murtih;
Pooja moolam guror padam;
Mantra moolam guror vakyam;
Moksha moolam guror kripa.

"The Guru's form should be meditated upon; the feet of the Guru should be worshipped; his words are to be treated as a sacred Mantra; his Grace ensures final liberation".

3. Sadhus and Sannyasins are then worshipped and fed at noon.

4. There is continuous Satsang during which discourses are held on the glory of devotion to the Guru in particular, and on spiritual topics in general.

5. Deserving aspirants are initiated into the Holy Order of Sannyas, as this is a highly auspicious occasion.

6. Devout disciples fast and spend the whole day in prayer. They also take fresh resolves for spiritual progress.

Wake up at Brahmamuhurta (at 4 a.m.) on this most holy day. Meditate on the lotus feet of your Guru. Mentally pray to him for his Grace, through which alone you can attain Self-realisation. Do vigorous Japa and meditate in the early morning hours.

After bath, worship the lotus feet of your Guru, or his image or picture with flowers, fruits, incense and camphor.

Fast or take only milk and fruits the whole day.

In the afternoon, sit with other devotees of your Guru and discuss with them the glories and teachings of your Guru.

Alternatively, you may observe the vow of silence and study the books or writings of your Guru, or mentally reflect upon his teachings.

Take fresh resolves on this holy day, to tread the spiritual path in accordance with the precepts of your Guru.

At night, assemble again with other devotees, and sing the Names of the Lord and the glories of your Guru.

The best form of worship of the Guru is to follow his teachings, to shine as the very embodiment of his teachings, and to propagate his glory and his message.

6

Holi

IN DAYS of yore, there were communities of cannibals in India. They did much havoc. They threatened the lives of many innocent people. One of them was Holika or Putana. She took immense delight in devouring children. Lord Krishna destroyed her and thus saved the little children. The effigy or figure of Holika is burnt in the fire up to this day. In South India, the figure of Cupid made of clay is burnt. This is the origin of the great festival of Holi.

It commences about ten days before the full moon of the month, Phalgun (February-March), but is usually only observed for the last three or four days, terminating with the full moon. This is a spring festival of the Hindus. In the spring season all the trees are filled with sweet smelling flowers. They all proclaim the glory and everlasting beauty of God and inspire you with hope, joy and a new life and stir you on to find out the Creator and the Indweller, who is hiding Himself in these forms.

Holi is known by the name of Kamadahana in South India, the day on which Cupid was burnt by Lord Shiva.

Another legend has it that once upon a time an old woman's grandchild was to be sacrificed to a female demon named Holika. A Sadhu advised her that abuse and foul language would subdue Holika. The old woman collected many children and made them abuse Holika with foul language. The demon fell dead on the ground. The children made a bonfire of her remains.

Connected to this Holika-legend is Bhakta Prahlad's devotion to Lord Narayana and his subsequent escape from death at the hands of Holika. Prahlad's father, Hiranyakashipu, punished him in a variety of ways to change his devotional mind and make him worldly-minded. He failed in all his attempts. At last he ordered his sister, Holika, who had a boon to remain unburnt even inside fire, to take Prahlad on her lap and enter into the blazing flames of the fire. Holika did so. She vanished, but Prahlad remained, laughing. He was not affected by the fire on account of the Grace of Lord Narayana.

This same scene is enacted every year to remind people that those who love God shall be saved and they that torture the devotee of God shall be reduced to ashes. When Holika was burnt, people abused her and sang praises of the Lord and His great devotee, Prahlad. In imitation of that, people even today use abusive language, but unfortunately forget to sing the praise of the Lord and His devotee!

In North India, people play joyfully with coloured water. The uncle pumps coloured water on the face and the body of his nephew. The niece applies coloured powder on the face of her aunt. Brothers play with sisters and cousins.

Huge bundles of wood are gathered and burnt at night, and everywhere one hears the shouts of "Holi-ho! Holi-ho!" People stand in the streets and pump coloured water over the body and clothes of any man who passes by, be he a rich man or an officer. There is no restriction on this day. It is like the April Fool day of the Europeans. People compose and sing special Holi songs.

During the festival, people clean their houses, remove all dirty articles around the house and burn them. The disease-breeding bacteria are thereby destroyed. The sanitary condition of the locality is improved. During the festival boys dance about in the streets. People play practical jokes with the passers-by. A bonfire is lit towards the close of the festival. Games representing the frolics of the young Krishna take place around the fire.

On the last day of Holi, people take a little fire from this bonfire, to their houses. They believe that their houses are rendered pure and free from disease.

Nowadays, people are found to indulge in all sorts of vices in the name of the Holi festival. Some drink intoxicating liquors like toddy and fall unconscious on the roads. They indulge in obscene speech as a result of drinking. They lose respect for their elders and masters. They waste their money in drink and dice-play. These evils should be totally eradicated.

Festivals like the Holi have their own spiritual value.

Apart from the various amusements, they create faith in God when properly observed. Hindu festivals always have a spiritual significance. They wean the man away from sensual pleasures and take him gradually to the spiritual path and divine communion. People perform *havan* and offer the new grains that are harvested to the gods before using them.

There should be worship of God, religious gatherings and Kirtan of the Lord's Names on such occasions, not mere pumping of coloured water and lighting bonfires. These functions are to be considered sacred and spent in devotional prayers, visiting holy places, bathing in sacred waters, Satsang with great evolved souls, doing charity to the poor, etc. Then only can Holi be said to have been properly celebrated. The devotees of the Lord remember the delightful pastimes of the Lord on such happy occasions.

All great Hindu festivals have religious, social and hygienic elements in them. Holi is no exception. Every season has a festival of its own. Holi is the great spring festival of India. Being an agricultural country India's two big festivals are at harvest time when the barns and granaries of our farmers are full and they have reason to enjoy the fruits of their hard labour. The harvest season is a festive season all over the world.

Man wants relaxation and change after hard work. He should be cheered up when he is depressed on account of work and anxieties. Festivals like these supply him with the real food and tonic to restore his cheer and peace of mind.

Holi

The religious element in the Holi festival is the worship of Krishna. In some places it is also called the Dol Yatra. The word *dol* literally means "a swing". An image of Krishna as a babe is placed in a little swing-cradle, and decorated with flowers and painted with coloured powders. The innocent frolics of little Krishna with the merry milkmaids (Gopis) of Brindavan are commemorated. Religious people chant the Name of Krishna and sing Holi-songs relating to the frolics of little Krishna with the Gopis.

The social element in Holi is the uniting or "embracing" of the great and the small, of the rich and the poor, and also amongst the equals. The festival teaches us to "let the dead bury the dead". Forget the outgoing year's ill-feelings and begin the new year with love, sympathy, co-operation and equality with all. Try to feel this oneness or unity with the Self also.

Holi also means "sacrifice". Burn all the impurities of the mind such as egoism, vanity, lust, etc., through the fire of devotion and knowledge. Ignite cosmic love, mercy, generosity, selflessness, truthfulness and purity through the fire of Yogic practice. This is the real spirit of Holi. Get up from the mire of stupidity and absurdity and dive deep into the ocean of divinity.

The call of Holi is to keep always the blaze of God-love shining in your heart. Inner spiritual illumination is real Holi. The spring season is the manifestation of the Lord, according to the *Bhagavad Gita*. Holi is there said to be His heart.

7

Kartigai Deepam

ON THE full moon day of the month of Kartigai (November-December) which falls on the ascension of the Kritigai star, the Hindus celebrate the Kartigai Deepam. It is on this day that the huge beacon is lit on the holy hill Arunachala, in South India.

Once Lord Shiva assumed the form of a hill at Tiruvannamalai in South India. Here He quelled the pride of Brahma and Vishnu who were quarelling as to their relative greatness. One day, when Lord Shiva was in meditation, Parvati left Him and went to the hill of Arunachala. There She performed penance. She was the guest of the sage Gautama. It was during Her penance here that Mahishasura was killed by Durga hidden by Parvati. Parvati saw Shiva as Arunacha-lesvara. She was taken back by the Lord to His side, and made His Ardhangini once more, that is, She occupied half of the body of the Lord.

Arunachalesvara is Tejo Lingam. Arunachala or the Tiruvannamalai Hill is the place that represents the fire element. (The five elements are represented by five holy places in India.)

Kartigai Deepam

When the light on the top of the Tiruvannamalai Hill is unveiled on the Kartigai Deepam day, people see the big light and worship it. They recite again and again in a loud voice "Harohara". The esoteric meaning is that he who sees the light of lights that is burning eternally in the chambers of his heart through constant meditation attains immortality. The light on the Arunachala brings the message to you that the Self or Lord Shiva is self-effulgent, He is the light of lights.

On the Kartigai Deepam day in South India, people make bonfires in front of temples in the evening. It is said that Lord Shiva burnt the chariots of several demons who were torturing sages and celestials. This bonfire symbolises this legend.

People place rows of earthen lamps in front of their houses on the evening of Kartigai Deepam and worship the Lord. They also light a variety of fireworks.

Annihilate the three impurities, namely, egoism, selfish action and delusion. Burn the mind, senses and the desires in the fire of knowledge of the Self or Shiva-Jnanam. Attain full illumination and behold the light of lights, which illumines the mind, intellect, sun, moon, stars, lightning and the fire. This is real Kartigai Deepam.

May the light of lights illumine you all! May Lord Shiva bless you with more light! May you merge in this supreme light and attain the eternal abode of bliss and immortality!

8

Makara Shankranti

SALUTATIONS to the Supreme Lord, the primordial Power that divided the year into the four seasons. Salutations to Surya the Sun-God who on this great day embarks on His northward journey.

The Sanskrit word "Shankramana" means "to begin to move". The day on which the sun begins to move northwards is called Makara Shankranti. It usually falls in the middle of January.

Among the Tamilians in South India this festival is called the Pongal.

To many people, especially the Tamilians, the Makara Shankranti ushers in the New Year. The newly-harvested corn is cooked for the first time on that day. Joyous festivities mark the celebration in every home. Servants, farmers and the poor are fed and clothed, and given presents of money. On the next day the cow, which is regarded as the symbol of the Holy Mother, is worshipped. Then there is feeding of birds and animals.

In this manner the devotee's heart gradually expands during the course of the celebrations, first embracing with its long arms of love the entire household and neighbours, then the servants and the poor, then the cow and then all other living creatures. Without even being conscious of it, one develops the heart, and expands it to such proportions that the entire universe finds a place in it.

As Shankranti is also the beginning of the month, Brahmins offer oblations to departed ancestors. Thus all the great sacrifices enjoined upon man, find their due place in this grand celebration. The worship of the cosmic form of the Lord is so well introduced into this that every man and woman in India is delightfully led to partake of it without even being aware of it.

To aspirants all over the world this day has a special significance. The six-month period during which the sun travels northwards is highly favourable to aspirants for their march towards the goal of life. It is as though the aspirant were flowing easily with the current towards the Supreme. Paramahamsa Sannyasins roam about freely during this period, dispelling gloom from the hearts of all. Devas and Rishis rejoice at the advent of the new season and readily come to the aid of the aspirant.

The great Bhishma, the grandfather of the Pandavas, who was fatally wounded during the Mahabharata war, waited on his death-bed of nails for the onset of this season before finally departing from the earth plane. Let us on this great day pay our homage to him and strive to become men of firm resolve ourselves!

As already mentioned, this is the Pongal festival in

South India. It is closely connected with agriculture. To the agriculturalist, it is a day of triumph. He would have by then brought home the fruit of his toils. Symbolically, the first harvest is offered to the Almighty—and that is Pongal. To toil was his task, his duty, but the fruit is now offered to Him—that is the spirit of Karma Yoga.

The master is not allowed to grab all the harvest for himself either. Pongal is the festival during which the landlord distributes food, clothes and money among the labourers who work under him. What a noble act!—an ideal you should constantly keep before you, not only ceremoniously on the Pongal day but at all times.

Be charitable. Be generous. Treat your servants as your bosom-friends and brother workers. This is the keynote of the Pongal festival. Thus would you earn their loyalty and enduring love.

The day prior to the Makara Shankranti, is called the Bhogi festival. On this day, old, worn-out and dirty things are discarded and burnt. Houses are cleaned and white-washed. Even the roads are swept clean and lovely designs are drawn with rice-flour. These practices have their own significance from the point of view of health. But, here I remind you that it will not do to attend to these external things alone. Cleaning the mind of its old dirty habits of thinking and feeling is more urgently needed. Burn them up with a wise and firm resolve to tread the path of truth, love and purity from this holy day onwards. That is the significance of Pongal in the life of the spiritual aspirant.

If you do this, then the Makara Shankranti has a special significance for you. For the sun, symbolising knowledge, wisdom and spiritual light, which receded from you when you revelled in the darkness of ignorance, delusion and sensuality, now joyously turns on its northward course and rushes towards you, to shed its light and warmth in greater abundance upon you and to infuse into you more life and energy.

In fact the sun itself symbolises all that the Pongal festival stands for. The message of the sun is the message of light, the message of unity, of impartiality, of true selflessness, of the perfection of the elements of Karma Yoga. The sun shines on all equally, it is the true benefactor of all beings. Without the sun life would perish on earth. It is extremely regular and punctual in its duties and never claims a reward or crave for recognition. If you imbibe these virtues of the sun, what doubt is there that you will shine with equal divine lustre!

He who dwells in the sun, whom the sun does not know, whose body the sun is and by whose power the sun shines, He is the Supreme Self, the Indweller, the immortal Essence. *Tat Twam Asi*—"That thou art". Realise this and be free, here and now, on this holy Pongal or Makara Shankranti day. This is my humble Pongal prayer to you all.

On the Shankranti day, sweets, puddings and sweet rice are prepared in every home, especially in South India. The pot in which the rice is cooked is beautifully adorned with tumeric leaves and roots, the symbols of auspiciousness. This cooking itself is done by the ladies of the household with great faith and devotion, feeling from the bottom of their hearts that it is an offering unto the Lord. When the milk in the pot in which the rice is cooked boils over, the ladies and the children get round the pot and shout "Pongalo Pongal!" with great joy and devotion. Special prayers are offered in the temples and houses. Then the people of the household gather together and eat in an air of love and festivity.

There is family re-union in all homes. Brothers renew their contact with married sisters who have gone away to live with the husband, by giving the sisters some presents.

The farmer is lovingly greeted by the landlord and is given presents of grains, clothes and money.

On the next day, the herds of cows are adorned beautifully, fed and worshipped. In some villages the youths demonstrate their valour by taking "the bull by the horn" (and often win their bride!). It is a great day for the cattle.

On the same day, young girls prepare various special dishes—sweet rice, sour rice, rice with coconut—and take them to the bank of a river or tank. They lay some leaves on the ground and place on them balls of the various preparations for the fish, birds and other creatures. It is an extremely colourful ceremony. The crows come down in large numbers and partake of the food. All the time the valuable lesson is driven into our minds: "Share what you have with all". The crow will call others before beginning to eat!

Makara Shankranti

Both these days, which are family re-union days, are regarded as being inauspicious for travel. This is to prevent us from going away from home on those days.

When you celebrate the Shankranti or Pongal in this manner, your sense of values changes. You begin to understand that your real wealth is the goodwill and friendship of your relatives, friends, neighbours, and servants; that your real wealth is the land on which your food grows, and the cattle which help you in agriculture and the cow which gives you milk. You begin to have greater love and respect for them and for all living beings—the crows, the fish and all other creatures.

In Maharashtra and in North India, spiritual aspirants attach much importance to Makara Shankranti. It is the season chosen by the Guru for bestowing his Grace on the disciple. In the South, too, it should be noted that it was about this time that Mahadeva favoured several of the Rishis by blessing them with His beatific vision.

9

Raksha Bandhan

RAKSHA BANDHAN is called Avani Avittam in South India. This falls on the full moon day of the month of Sravan (August-September). It is an important Hindu festival. Hindus wear a new holy thread and offer libations of water to the ancient Rishis on this day.

Recitation of the *Vedas* on this great day is highly beneficial. This festival is also known as Upakarmam, and is specially sacred to the Brahmins who have been invested with the sacred thread. When the Brahmin boy is invested with this holy thread, symbolically his third eye or the eye of wisdom is opened. This festival of Upakarmam reminds the wearer of the sacred thread of its glorious spiritual significance. Brahmins also offer libations with water to their ancestors to whom they owe their birth and to the Rishis to whom they are indebted for their spiritual knowledge and the *Vedas* themselves. The true Hindu never forgets his benefactors!

The followers of the four different *Vedas* have their Upakarmam on different days.

On this day, Sachi, the consort of Indra, tied a holy

thread or amulet around the wrist of Indra when he was defeated by the demons. Then Indra, the king of gods, gained a victory over the demons, by the power of this protection (Raksha means "protection") and recovered the lost city of Amaravati.

In North India, on this day, an amulet known as a Rakshi or Rakhi, is tied round the wrist of brothers by the sisters as a protection from evil during the ensuing year. Brahmins and Purohits similarly tie amulets round the wrists of their patrons and receive gifts. A Mantra is recited when the Rakhi or the silken thread is tied. The silken thread is charged with the power of the Mantra which is as follows:

Yena baddho balee raajaa daanavendro mahaabalah;
Tena twaam anubadhnaami rakshey maa chala maa chala.

The power of this Mantra protects the wearer from evil influences.

Ratha Saptami

THIS FALLS on the 7th day of the bright fortnight of the month of Margaseersha (December-January). People worship the sun in the early morning and recite the *Surya Sahasranama*. Good actions done on this day give manifold results. Brahmins become celestials if they fast on this day and worship God; Kshatriyas, that is, people of the warrior caste, become Brahmins; Vaishyas, the merchants, become Kshatriyas: and Sudras or men of the servant caste, become Vaishyas. If women fast on this day, they attain knowledge and derive virtues. If widows fast on this day, they get rid of widowhood from the next birth onwards. Even the sin of slaying a Brahmin is expiated by the power of fasting on this day. He who takes a bath at the time of sunrise is purified like Mother Ganges. He can never become a poor man.

Fast on this day. Observe the vow of silence. Remain in a solitary place. Do Japa. Practise intense meditation with faith and devotion. You are sure to attain God-realisation on this very day!

Telugu New Year's Day

THIS FALLS on the first day of the month of Chaitra (March-April) according to Chandramana. This is a day of rejoicing. This is new year's day for the people of Andhra Pradesh and also the Telugu people all over the world.

Those who live north of the Vindhya hills observe Barhaspatyamana. Those living south of the Vindhya hills observe Sauramana or Chandramana.

There is a peculiarity about the practices of the various sects of Brahmins; one who is not conversant with them finds it difficult to understand their meaning. Even though they are all Brahmins, certain differences in their lineage may be traced among them. These become manifest in their distinctive calendars where the dates and months vary. Some have calculations according to the solar system, and others according to the lunar system, with the result that despite all being Brahmins, the New Year differs among different sects. Thus there is a Telugu New Year's Day, a Tamil New Year's Day, and a New Year's Day distinct from these in the almanac of North India.

Vasanta Navaratri

THE DIVINE MOTHER or Devi is worshipped during the Vasanta Navaratri. This occurs during the spring. She is worshipped by Her own command. You will find this in the following episode in the *Devi Bhagavata*.

In days long gone by, King Dhruvasindu was killed by a lion when he went out hunting. Preparations were made to crown the prince Sudarsana. But, King Yudhajit of Ujjain, the father of Queen Lilavati, and King Virasena of Kalinga, the father of Queen Manorama, were each desirous of securing the Kosala throne for their respective grandsons. They fought with each other. King Virasena was killed in the battle. Manorama fled to the forest with Prince Sudarsana and a eunuch. They took refuge in the hermitage of Rishi Bharadwaja.

The victor, King Yudhajit, thereupon crowned his grandson, Satrujit, at Ayodhya, the capital of Kosala. He then went out in search of Manorama and her son. The Rishi said that he would not give up those who had sought protection under him. Yudhajit became furious.

He wanted to attack the Rishi. But, his minister told him about the truth of the Rishi's statement. Yudhajit returned to his capital.

Fortune smiled on Prince Sudarsana. A hermit's son came one day and called the eunuch by his Sanskrit name Kleeba. The prince caught the first syllable *Kli* and began to pronounce it as *Kleem*. This syllable happened to be a powerful, sacred Mantra. It is the Bija Akshara (root syllable) of the Divine Mother. The prince obtained peace of mind and the Grace of the Divine Mother by the repeated utterance of this syllable. Devi appeared to him, blessed him and granted him divine weapons and an inexhaustible quiver.

The emissaries of the king of Benares passed through the Ashram of the Rishi and, when they saw the noble prince Sudarsana, they recommended him to Princess Sashikala, the daughter of the king of Benares.

The ceremony at which the princess was to choose her spouse was arranged. Sashikala at once chose Sudarsana. They were duly wedded. King Yudhajit, who had been present at the function, began to fight with the king of Benares. Devi helped Sudarsana and his father-in-law. Yudhajit mocked Her, upon which Devi promptly reduced Yudhajit and his army to ashes.

Thus Sudarsana, with his wife and his father-in-law, praised Devi. She was highly pleased and ordered them to perform Her worship with *havan* and other means during the Vasanta Navaratri. Then She disappeared.

Prince Sudarsana and Sashikala returned to the Ashram of Rishi Bharadwaja. The great Rishi blessed them and crowned Sudarsana as the king of Kosala. Sudarsana and Sashikala and the king of Benares implicitly carried out the commands of the Divine Mother and performed worship in a splendid manner during the Vasanta Navaratri.

Sudarsana's descendants, namely, Sri Rama and Lakshmana, also performed worship of Devi during the Vasanta Navaratri and were blessed with Her assistance in the recovery of Sita.

It is the devout Hindu's duty to perform the worship of Devi for both material and spiritual welfare during the Vasanta Navaratri and follow the noble example set by Sudarsana and Sri Rama. He cannot achieve anything without the Divine Mother's blessings. So, sing Her praise and repeat Her Mantra and Name. Meditate on Her form. Do worship. Pray and obtain Her eternal Grace and blessings. May the Divine Mother bless you with all divine wealth!

13

Vasanta Panchami

THIS IS an important bathing day. All Hindus observe it. It is also known as Magh Sukla Panchami as it falls in the month of Magh (January-February). This is the festival that marks the first day of spring.

Vasanta means the spring season, which is very congenial for doing vigorous Yoga Sadhana.

Men, women and girls wear yellow cloth. The yellow colour is a sign of auspiciousness and spirituality. It represents the ripening of the spring crops. Even the food is coloured yellow by using saffron. All the folk get together and sing songs connected with spring.

All get up in the early morning, take bath and worship the sun, Mother Ganga, the Deity of the sacred river Ganges, and the earth.

On this memorable day, Lord Shiva burnt the god of love, Cupid. The gods had sent Cupid to tempt the Lord while he was absorbed in Samadhi, in order to beget a powerful son who would be able to destroy the wicked demon Tarakasura. Cupid discharged an arrow at Lord Shiva from behind a tree. Shiva became very greatly enraged. He opened His third eye and reduced

Cupid to ashes. More details of this story are given in the chapter on Skanda Sashti.

The Bengalis call this festival Saraswathi Puja. They worship the Goddess Saraswathi on this day. The image of the Goddess is taken in procession and immersed in the holy Ganges.

14

Sri Appayya Jayanthi

SRI APPAYYA Dikshita was born in the Krishna Paksha of the Kanya month of Pramateecha Varsha (1544 A.D.) on the auspicious hour and day under the Uttaraproshtapada constellation. His Jayanthi is celebrated every year on 2nd October.

Sri Appayya, the greatest name in the 16th century annals of South India, is the reputed author of more than 104 books, representative of all branches of knowledge in Sanskrit literature. He attained greatness mainly by his works on Vedanta. All the schools of Vedanta have drawn unique and unrivalled authority and support from his pen.

Of his Vedantic works, the *Chaturmata Sara Sangrah* is justly famous for the impartial justice with which he has expounded the tenets of the four great schools, namely, the Dwaita, Visishtadwaita, Shivadwaita and the Adwaita. This exposition is given in his *Nyaya Muktavali, Nyaya Mukhamalika, Nyaya Manimala,* and *Nyaya Manjari* (all these together form the *Chaturmata Sara Sangrah*).

In almost all branches of Sanskrit learning and

literature—poetry, rhetoric, philosophy—his name was peerless among his contemporaries, or for that matter, for decades after him and till today. His *Kuvalayananda* is generally the first work of rhetoric that is taken up for study. As is usual, Pundit Jagannatha, his contemporary and rival, levelled some criticism on it in his *Rasagangadhara.*

His poems in praise of Lord Shiva are great favourites among the worshippers of Shiva. He has also written a learned commentary entitled *Parimalam* on Vedanta; this is an outstanding monument of his philosophic erudition.

He had a gigantic intellect. Great was the reverence paid to him in his own lifetime; even today he is greatly revered. Once he went to the village which was the birthplace of his wife. A grand reception was accorded to him by the villagers who were proud of calling him one of themselves. There was great excitement. All hailed him with the words, "The great Dikshita is coming amongst us!". There was no other talk among the villagers for days before the event. The day came, and the distinguished guest, Appayya Dikshita, was greeted by crowds of people who flocked to have a sight of the grand lion of learning.

An old lady, curious to a degree, came out, staff in hand, to see the phenomenon; with the freedom that is conceded to one of her age, she made her way easily through the crowd and looked at him steadily for some minutes. Dim recollections of a face, floated in her mind.

Definitely recalling the face, she exclaimed, "I have seen this face somewhere. Wait. Oh yes! are you not the husband of Achha?"

The great scholar confirmed her surmise with a smile.

The good old lady was disappointed. With her face and spirits fallen, she retraced her steps homeward, remarking, "What ado to make—just over Achha's husband!"

Appayya summarised a world of wisdom when he perpetuated the incident in a half verse: "Asmin grame achha prasiddha—In this village the name and precedence are Achha's!"

Appayya is considered as an Avatara of Lord Shiva. When he went to Tirupati temple in South India, the Vaishnavas refused him admission. The next morning they found the Vishnu *murti* in the temple changed into a Shiva *murti*. The spiritual head of the temple was most astonished and startled. He begged pardon and prayed to Appayya to restore the original form of Vishnu.

Appayya flourished in the middle of the 16th century. He was a great rival of Pundit Jagannatha in the field of poetry. Appayya had no independent views on the doctrinal side of Shankara's Vedanta, but carried on fierce controversies with the followers of Vallabha at Jaipur and other places. He summarised his views in the *Siddhantalesha*, which is the most admirable digest of the doctrinal differences among the followers of Shankara.

No doubt, he is among the greatest of the spiritual luminaries that India has produced. Though a detailed account of the history of his life is lacking, his works are sufficient testimony of his greatness.

On this great day (2nd October) when you celebrate the birthday of Appayya Dikshita, pray and worship the Lord and your Guru. Study Appayya's works, especially his great devotional work, *Atmarpana Stuthi*.

15

Dattatreya Jayanthi

Om Namo Bhagavate Dattatreyaya

DATTATREYA Jayanthi falls during December-January on the full moon day of the month of Margaseersha. His story is told as follows.

Anusuya is quoted as the model of chastity. She was the wife of Atri Maharishi, a great sage and one of the seven foremost seers and sages. She was well established in the Pativrata Dharma, the main elements of which are devotion to husband and regard of him as God Himself. She did severe austerities for a very long time in order to beget sons equal to Brahma, Vishnu and Shiva, the Hindu Trinity.

Once, Saraswathi, Lakshmi and Parvati requested their husbands (the Trimurtis) to test the Pativrata Dharma of Anusuya, by asking her to give them alms with an unclothed body.

Brahma, Vishnu and Shiva came to know of the austerity and desire of Anusuya. So, they agreed to their wives' request, as they knew that by agreeing to it, they would also be fulfilling Anusuya's wish. They put on the garb of Sannyasins and appeared before Anusuya, asking her to give them alms as specified by their wives. Anusuya was in a great dilemma. She could not say "No" to the Sannyasins. And she had to maintain her Pativrata Dharma also, which she would be violating if she appeared naked before men other than her own husband. She meditated on the form of her husband, took refuge at his feet and sprinkled over the three Sannyasins a few drops of water used for washing the feet of her husband. Immediately the Trimurtis were transformed into three babies on account of the glory of her chastity. At the same time, there was accumulation of milk in her breast. She thought that these children were her own and fed them with the milk, in a nude state and cradled them. She was eagerly expecting the arrival of her husband who had gone to have a bath.

As soon as Atri Rishi returned home, Anusuya related all that had happened during his absence, placed the three children at his feet and worshipped him. But, Atri knew all this already through his divine vision. He embraced all the three children. They became one child, with two feet, one trunk, three heads and six hands. Atri Rishi blessed his wife and informed her that the Trimurtis themselves had assumed the forms of the three children to gratify her wish.

In the meantime, Narada went to Saraswathi, Lakshmi and Parvati and informed them that their husbands had been turned into children through the power of the Pativrata Dharma of Anusuya and that they would not return unless they asked for their husbands as alms from Rishi Atri. Thus Saraswathi, Lakshmi and Parvati assumed the form of ordinary women, appeared before Atri and asked for their own husbands as alms. Atri duly honoured the three ladies and, with folded palms, prayed to them that his wish and the wish of Anusuya should be fulfilled.

Then, the Trimurtis appeared in their true form before Atri and said, "This child will be a great sage according to your word and will be equal to us, according to the wish of Anusuya. The child will bear the name of Dattatreya." Saying this they disappeared.

The child Dattatreya soon attained manhood. As he had the rays of the Trimurtis and as he was a great man of the highest wisdom, all the Rishis and ascetics worshipped him. He was gentle, peaceful and amiable. He was an Avadhuta—an ascetic who always remains naked. He preached the Truth of Vedanta. Dattatreya taught his *Avadhuta Gita* to Lord Subramanya. This is a wonderful book which contains the truths and secrets of Vedanta and the experiences of Self-realisation.

Once, while he was roaming happily in a forest, he met King Yadu, who, on seeing Dattatreya so happy, asked him the secret of his happiness and the name of his Guru.

Dattatreya said, "The Self alone is my Guru. Yet, I have learnt wisdom from twenty-four other individuals and objects. So they, too, are also my Gurus."

Dattatreya then mentioned the names of his twenty-four Gurus and spoke of the wisdom that he had learnt from each as follows:

"The names of my twenty-four Gurus are earth, water, fire, sky, moon, sun, pigeon, python, ocean, moth, honey-gatherers (black bee), bees, elephant, deer, fish, the dancing-girl Pingala, raven, child, maiden, serpent, arrow-maker, spider and beetle.

1. I learnt patience and doing good to others from the *earth*.

2. From *water*, I learnt the quality of purity.

3. I learnt from *air* to be without attachment though I move with many people in this world.

4. From *fire* I learnt to glow with the splendour of Self-knowledge and austerity.

5. I learnt from the *sky* that the Self is all-pervading and yet it has no contact with any object.

6. I learnt from the *moon* that the Self is always perfect and changeless and it is only the limiting adjuncts that cast shadows over it.

7. Just as a sun reflected in various pots of water appears as so many different reflections, so also Brahman appears different because of the bodies caused by the reflection through the mind. This is the lesson I have learnt from the *sun*.

8. I once saw a pair of *pigeons* with their young birds. A fowler spread a net and caught the young birds. The mother pigeon was very much attached to her children. She fell into the net and was caught. From this I have learnt that attachment is the root cause of earthly bondage.

9. The *python* does not move about for its food. It remains contented with whatever it gets, lying in one

LORD DATTATREYA
Who is regarded as an Incarnation of the Trinity.

place. From this I learnt to be unmindful of food and to be contented with whatever I get to eat.

10. Just as the *ocean* remains unmoved, even though hundreds of rivers flow into it, so also the wise man should remain unmoved among all the various sorts of temptations, difficulties and troubles.

11. To control the sense of sight and to fix the mind on the Self, is the lesson I learnt from the *moth*.

12. I take a little food from one house and a little from another house and thus appease my hunger. I am not a burden on the householder. This I learnt from the *black bee* which gathers honey from various flowers.

13. *Bees* collect honey with great trouble, but a hunter comes along and takes the honey away easily. From this I learnt that it is useless to hoard things.

14. The male *elephant*, blinded by lust, falls into a pit covered with grass, even at the sight of a female elephant. Therefore, one should destroy lust.

15. The *deer* is enticed and trapped by the hunter through its love of music. Therefore, one should never listen to lewd songs.

16. Just as a *fish* that is covetous of food falls an easy victim to the bait, so also the man who is greedy for food loses his independence and easily gets ruined.

17. There was a *dancing girl* named Pingala. Being tired of looking for customers, one night she became hopeless. She had to be contented with what traffic she had that day and retired to a sound sleep. I learnt from this fallen woman the lesson that the abandonment of hope leads to contentment.

18. A *raven* picked up a piece of flesh. It was pursued and beaten by other birds. It dropped the piece of flesh and attained peace and rest. From this I learnt that a man in the world undergoes all sorts of troubles and miseries when he runs after sensual pleasures and that he becomes as happy as the bird when he abandons them.

19. The *child* who sucks milk is free from all cares, worries and anxieties, and is always cheerful. I learnt the virtue of cheerfulness from the child.

20. The *maiden* was husking paddy. Her bangles made much noise and there were visitors from her husband's house. To silence the bangles, she removed them, one by one. Even when there were just two, they produced some noise. When she had only one, it did not make any noise, and she was happy. I learnt from the maiden that living among many would create discord, disturbance, dispute and quarrel. Even among two there might be unnecessary words or strife. The ascetic or the Sannyasin should remain alone in solitude.

21. A *serpent* does not build its own hole. It dwells in the holes dug out by others. Even so, an ascetic should not build a home for himself. He should live in a temple or a cave built by others.

22. I learnt from the *arrow-maker* the quality of intense concentration of mind.

23. The *spider* pours out of its mouth long threads and weaves them into cobwebs. Then it gets itself entangled in the net of its own making. Even so, man makes a net of his own ideas and gets entangled in it.

The wise man should, therefore, abandon all worldly thoughts and think of Brahman only.

24. The *beetle* catches hold of a worm, puts it in its nest and gives it a sting. The poor worm, always fearing the return of the beetle and sting, and thinking constantly of the beetle, becomes a beetle itself. I learnt from the beetle and the worm to turn myself into the Self by contemplating constantly on It; thus I gave up all attachment to the body and attained liberation."

The king was highly impressed by listening to these enlightening words of Lord Dattatreya. He abandoned the world and practised constant meditation on the Self.

Dattatreya was absolutely free from intolerance or prejudice of any kind. He learnt wisdom from whatever source it came. All seekers after wisdom should follow the example of Dattatreya.

On Dattatreya Jayanthi, get up at Brahmamuhurta and meditate. Fast and pray throughout the day. Do not mix with anybody. Live in total seclusion. Forget the body. Identify yourself with the blissful Self. Study Dattatreya's glorious works, namely, the *Avadhuta Gita* and the *Jivanmukta Gita*. Worship Lord Dattatreya's (or, your own Guru's) form. Take wholesome resolves that you will follow the great teachings of Lord Dattatreya. You will realise the Self very soon.

At the Sivananda Ashram, Rishikesh, this day is celebrated every year on a grand scale, in the Dattatreya Temple, on a hillock near the main Ashram.

1. The glorious Image of Lord Dattatreya is duly worshipped, with bathing and flowers.

2. All the spiritual aspirants assemble there, singing the Lord's Names and glories.

3. Discourses are given by Yogis and Sannyasins, on the life and teachings of Lord Dattatreya during this gathering as well as during the night Satsang at the Ashram. The *Avadhuta Gita* and the *Jivanmukta Gita* are also read and explained.

4. It is a day of great rejoicing.

May you all enjoy the choicest blessings of Lord Dattatreya, and may you all attain the highest goal, Self-realisation in this very birth!

16

Ganesh Chaturthi

SALUTATIONS to Lord Ganesha who is Brahman Himself, who is the Supreme Lord, who is the energy of Lord Shiva, who is the source of all bliss, and who is the bestower of all virtuous qualities and success in all undertakings.

> *Mushikavaahana modaka hastha,*
> *Chaamara karna vilambitha sutra,*
> *Vaamana rupa maheshwara putra,*
> *Vighna vinaayaka paada namasthe*

MEANING: "O Lord Vinayaka! the remover of all obstacles, the son of Lord Shiva, with a form which is very short, with mouse as Thy vehicle, with sweet pudding in hand, with wide ears and long hanging trunk, I prostrate at Thy lotus-like Feet!"

Ganesh Chaturthi is one of the most popular of Hindu festivals. This is the birthday of Lord Ganesha. It is the day most sacred to Lord Ganesha. It falls on the 4th day of the bright fortnight of Bhadrapada (August-

September). It is observed throughout India, as well as by devoted Hindus in all parts of the world.

Clay figures of the Deity are made and after being worshipped for two days, or in some cases ten days, they are thrown into water.

Lord Ganesha is the elephant-headed God. He is worshipped first in any prayers. His Names are repeated first before any auspicious work is begun, before any kind of worship is begun.

He is the Lord of power and wisdom. He is the eldest son of Lord Shiva and the elder brother of Skanda or Kartikeya. He is the energy of Lord Shiva and so He is called the son of Shankar and Umadevi. By worshipping Lord Ganesha mothers hope to earn for their sons the sterling virtues of Ganesha.

The following story is narrated about His birth and how He came to have the head of an elephant:

Once upon a time, the Goddess Gauri (consort of Lord Shiva), while bathing, created Ganesha as a pure white being out of the mud of Her Body and placed Him at the entrance of the house. She told Him not to allow anyone to enter while she went inside for a bath. Lord Shiva Himself was returning home quite thirsty and was stopped by Ganesha at the gate. Shiva became angry and cut off Ganesha's head as He thought Ganesha was an outsider.

When Gauri came to know of this she was sorely grieved. To console her grief, Shiva ordered His servants to cut off and bring to Him the head of any creature that might be sleeping with its head facing north. The servants went on their mission and found only an elephant in that position. The sacrifice was thus made and the elephant's head was brought before Shiva. The Lord then joined the elephant's head onto the body of Ganesha.

Lord Shiva made His son worthy of worship at the beginning of all undertakings, marriages, expeditions, studies, etc. He ordained that the annual worship of Ganesha should take place on the 4th day of the bright half of Bhadrapada.

Without the Grace of Sri Ganesha and His help nothing whatsoever can be achieved. No action can be undertaken without His support, Grace or blessing.

In his first lesson in the alphabet a Maharashtrian child is initiated into the Mantra of Lord Ganesha, *Om Sri Ganeshaya Namah*. Only then is the alphabet taught.

The following are some of the common Names of Lord Ganesha: Dhoomraketu, Sumukha, Ekadantha, Gajakarnaka, Lambodara, Vignaraja, Ganadhyaksha, Phalachandra, Gajanana, Vinayaka, Vakratunda, Siddhivinayaka, Surpakarna, Heramba, Skandapurvaja, Kapila and Vigneshwara. He is also known by many as Maha-Ganapathi.

His Mantra is *Om Gung Ganapathaye Namah*. Spiritual aspirants who worship Ganesha as their tutelary Deity repeat this Mantra or *Om Sri Ganeshaya Namah*.

The devotees of Ganesha also do Japa of the Ganesha Gayatri Mantra. This is as follows.

Ganesh Chaturthi

Tat purushaaya vidmahe
Vakratundaaya dheemahi
Tanno dhanti prachodayaat.

Lord Ganesha is an embodiment of wisdom and bliss. He is the Lord of Brahmacharins. He is foremost amongst the celibates.

He has as his vehicle a small mouse. He is the presiding Deity of the Muladhara Chakra, the psychic centre in the body in which the Kundalini Shakti resides.

He is the Lord who removes all obstacles on the path of the spiritual aspirant, and bestows upon him worldly as well as spiritual success. Hence He is called Vigna Vinayaka. His Bija Akshara (root syllable) is *Gung*, pronounced to rhyme with the English word "sung". He is the Lord of harmony and peace.

Lord Ganesha represents Om or the Pranava, which is the chief Mantra among the Hindus. Nothing can be done without uttering it. This explains the practice of invoking Ganesha before beginning any rite or undertaking any project. His two feet represent the power of knowledge and the power of action. The elephant head is significant in that it is the only figure in nature that has the form of the symbol for Om.

The significance of riding on a mouse is the complete conquest over egoism. The holding of the *ankusha* represents His rulership of the world. It is the emblem of divine Royalty.

Ganesha is the first God. Riding on a mouse, one of

nature's smallest creatures and having the head of an elephant, the biggest of all animals, denotes that Ganesha is the creator of all creatures. Elephants are very wise animals; this indicates that Lord Ganesha is an embodiment of wisdom. It also denotes the process of evolution—the mouse gradually evolves into an elephant and finally becomes a man. This is why Ganesha has a human body, an elephant's head and a mouse as His vehicle. This is the symbolic philosophy of His form.

He is the Lord of Ganas or groups, for instance groups of elements, groups of senses, etc. He is the head of the followers of Shiva or the celestial servants of Lord Shiva.

The Vaishnavas also worship Lord Ganesha. They have given Him the name of Tumbikkai Alwar which means the divinity with the proboscis (the elephant's trunk).

Lord Ganesha's two powers are the Kundalini and the Vallabha or power of love.

He is very fond of sweet pudding or balls of rice flour with a sweet core. On one of His birthdays He was going around house to house accepting the offerings of sweet puddings. Having eaten a good number of these, He set out moving on His mouse at night. Suddenly the mouse stumbled—it had seen a snake and became frightened —with the result that Ganesha fell down. His stomach burst open and all the sweet puddings came out. But Ganesha stuffed them back into His stomach and, catching hold of the snake, tied it around His belly.

Seeing all this, the moon in the sky had a hearty laugh. This unseemly behaviour of the moon annoyed Him immensely and so he pulled out one of His tusks and hurled it against the moon, and cursed that no one should look at the moon on the Ganesh Chaturthi day. If anyone does, he will surely earn a bad name, censure or ill-repute. However, if by mistake someone does happen to look at the moon on this day, then the only way he can be freed from the curse is by repeating or listening to the story of how Lord Krishna cleared His character regarding the Syamantaka jewel. This story is quoted in the *Srimad Bhagavatam*. Lord Ganesha was pleased to ordain thus. Glory to Lord Ganesha! How kind and merciful He is unto His devotees!

Ganesha and His brother Lord Subramanya once had a dispute as to who was the elder of the two. The matter was referred to Lord Shiva for final decision. Shiva decided that whoever would make a tour of the whole world and come back first to the starting point had the right to be the elder. Subramanya flew off at once on his vehicle, the peacock, to make a circuit of the world. But the wise Ganesha went, in loving worshipfulness, around His divine parents and asked for the prize of His victory.

Lord Shiva said, "Beloved and wise Ganesha! But how can I give you the prize; you did not go around the world?"

Ganesha replied, "No, but I have gone around my parents. My parents represent the entire manifested universe!"

Thus the dispute was settled in favour of Lord Ganesha, who was thereafter acknowledged as the elder of the two brothers. Mother Parvati also gave Him a fruit as a prize for this victory.

In the *Ganapathi Upanishad*, Ganesha is identified with the Supreme Self. The legends that are connected with Lord Ganesha are recorded in the Ganesha Khanda of the *Brahma Vivartha Purana*.

On the Ganesh Chaturthi day, meditate on the stories connected with Lord Ganesha early in the morning, during the Brahmamuhurta period. Then, after taking a bath, go to the temple and do the prayers of Lord Ganesha. Offer Him some coconut and sweet pudding. Pray with faith and devotion that He may remove all the obstacles that you experience on the spiritual path. Worship Him at home, too. You can get the assistance of a pundit. Have an image of Lord Ganesha in your house. Feel His Presence in it.

Don't forget not to look at the moon on that day; remember that it behaved unbecomingly towards the Lord. This really means avoid the company of all those who have no faith in God, and who deride God, your Guru and religion, from this very day.

Take fresh spiritual resolves and pray to Lord Ganesha for inner spiritual strength to attain success in all your undertakings.

May the blessings of Sri Ganesha be upon you all! May He remove all the obstacles that stand in your spiritual path! May He bestow on you all material prosperity as well as liberation!

17

Gita Jayanthi

THE GITA Jayanthi or the birthday of the *Bhagavad Gita* is celebrated throughout India by all admirers and lovers of this sacred scripture on the 11th day (Ekadashi) of the bright half of the month of Margaseersha (December-January) according to the Hindu almanac. That was the day on which Sanjaya narrated the dialogue between Sri Krishna and Arjuna, to King Dhritarashtra, and thus made the glorious teachings of the Lord available to us, to all the people of the world, and for all time.

The Gita Jayanthi marks one of the greatest days in the history of mankind. Nearly six thousand years ago on that day a dazzling flash of brilliant lightning lit up the firmament of human civilization. That spiritual effulgence, that flash, was the message of the *Bhagavad Gita*, given by the Lord Himself on the battlefield of Kurukshetra. Unlike ordinary flashes of lightning which die away after flashing for a split-second, this brilliant flash of that memorable day continued to shine through the centuries and even now illumines the path of humanity on its onward march to perfection.

The *Gita* is the most beautiful and only truly philosophical song. It contains sublime lessons on wisdom and philosophy. It is the "Song Celestial". It is the universal gospel. It contains the message of life that appeals to all, irrespective of race, creed, age or religion.

The *Gita* was given to us about six thousand years ago through Arjuna, an Indian prince, by Sri Krishna, the Lord incarnate. The teachings are based on the *Upanishads*, the ancient, revealed metaphysical classics of India. The *Gita* shows a way to rise above the world of duality and the pairs of opposites and to attain eternal bliss and immortality. It is a gospel of action. It teaches the rigid performance of one's duty in society, the life of active struggle, keeping one's inner being untouched by outer surroundings and renouncing all fruits of actions as offerings unto the Lord.

The *Gita* is a source of power and wisdom. It strengthens you when you are weak and inspires you when you are feeble. It teaches you to embrace righteousness and resist unrighteousness.

The *Gita* is not merely a book; it is not a mere scripture. It is a living voice carrying an eternally vital and indispensable message to mankind. Its verses embody words of wisdom, coming from the infinite ocean of knowledge, the Absolute Itself.

The voice of the *Gita* is the call of the Supreme. It is the divine sound explained. The mightiest primal source of all existence, all power, is the manifested sound, Om. This is the divine Word. It is the Nada Brahman whose unceasing call is: "Be ye all ever merged in the eternal unbroken continuous consciousness of the Supreme Truth". This is the sublime message that the great *Gita* elaborates and presents in all comprehensiveness and in a universally accepted form. It is verily this message of the *Bhagavad Gita* that I wish to recall and reproclaim with emphasis to you.

To be always conscious of the Divine, to ever feel the Divine Presence, to live always in the awareness of the Supreme Being in the chambers of your heart and everywhere around you, is verily to live a life of fullness and divine perfection on earth itself. Such constant remembrance of God and such attitude of mind will release you forever from the clutches of Maya and free you from all fear. To forget the Supreme is to fall into Maya. To forget Him is to be assailed by fear. To live in unbroken remembrance of the Supreme Truth is to remain always in the region of Light, far beyond Maya's reach.

Mark carefully how the *Gita* again and again stresses upon this lofty message. The Lord declares: "Keep thou thy mind in Me, in Me place thy reason".

In another verse, He says: "Therefore, at all times remember Me and fight. You will surely attain Me, thus having offered yourself".

And yet again: "Perform action remaining united with Me at heart".

The *Gita* guides you to glory with the watchwords: "Be thou divine-minded, devoted to Me as your goal, and let your subconscious mind be divine".

The Lord gives the following firm assurance also: "I

become the saviour from this mortal world for those whose minds are set on Me".

Such is the most illuminating message of the *Gita*, seeking to lead man to a life of perfection even while performing his ordained role here. Long has this message been neglected by man. Forgetting the Lord, the world has turned towards sense-indulgence and mammon. A terrible price has been paid. O man! enough of this forgetfulness, for the Lord has amply warned man against heedlessness: "If, out of egoism, thou wilt not hear, then thou shalt perish".

It is a matter for great regret that many young men and women of India know very little of this unique scripture. You cannot consider yourself as having attained a good standard of education if you do not have a sound knowledge of the *Srimad Bhagavad Gita*. All post-graduate knowledge, all research in universities is mere husk or chaff when compared to the wisdom of the *Gita*.

Live in the spirit of the teachings of the *Gita*. Mere talk or lectures will not help you in any way. Become a practical "man-of-the-*Gita*".

The *Gita* may be summarised in these seven verses:

1. "Uttering the one-syllabled Om, the Brahman, and remembering Me, he who departs, leaving the body, attains the Supreme Goal".

2. "It is meet, O Lord, that the world delights and rejoices in Thy praise; the demons fly in fear to all quarters, and all the hosts of Siddhas bow to Thee!"

3. "With hands and feet everywhere, with eyes, heads and mouths everywhere, with ears everywhere, He exists in the world, enveloping all".

4. "Whosoever meditates on the omniscient, ancient Ruler of the whole world, minuter than an atom, the supporter of all, of form inconceivable, effulgent like the sun, he goeth beyond the darkness of ignorance".

5. "They, the wise, speak of the indestructible Asvattha, having its roots above and branches below, whose leaves are the metres or hymns; he who knows it is a knower of the *Vedas*".

6. "And I am seated in the hearts of all; from Me are memory, knowledge, as well as their absence. I am verily that which has to be known by all the *Vedas*; and I am indeed the author of the Vedanta and the knower of the *Vedas* am I".

7. "Fix thy mind on Me; be devoted to Me; sacrifice to Me; bow down to Me; having thus united thy whole Self to Me, taking Me as the Supreme Lord, thou shalt verily come to Me".

Read the whole *Gita* on Sundays and other holidays. Study again and again the verses in the Second Discourse which deal with the state of the Sthithaprajna (a perfected Yogi and sage). Also study the eight nectarine verses of the Twelfth Discourse.

The study of the *Gita* alone is sufficient for the purpose of scriptural study. You will find in it a solution to all your problems. The more you study it, with devotion and faith, the deeper will your knowledge become, the more penetrative would be your insight, and the clearer your thinking. Even if you live in the spirit of one verse of the *Gita* all your miseries will come to an end and you will attain the goal of life— immortality and eternal peace.

None but the Lord can bring out such an unprecedented and marvellous book, which bestows peace to its readers, which helps and guides them in the attainment of supreme bliss, and which has survived to this day.

The teachings of the *Gita* are broad, sublime and universal. Its teachings do not belong to any cult, sect, creed, particular age, place or country. Its teachings are for all. It teaches a method which is within the reach of all. It has a message for the solace, peace, freedom, salvation and perfection of all human beings.

At the Sivananda Ashram, Rishikesh, the auspicious Gita Jayanthi is observed every year on a grand scale:

1. All spiritual aspirants wake up at 4 a.m. and do meditation on the Lord.

2. From sunrise to sunset, there is unbroken recitation of the *Gita*. The Samputa-method is adopted, that is, before and after each verse of the *Gita*, the following Samputa is recited.

Sarva dharmam parityajya maamekam sharanam vraja;
Aham twa sarvapaapebhyo mokshayishyaami ma sucha.

Thus, between two verses of the *Gita*, this verse is recited twice. This is an extremely efficacious method of earning the Grace of the Lord and the *Gita*, the Mother.

3. All spiritual aspirants fast the whole day (it is also Ekadashi).

4. Various competitions' are held, especially for small children to manifest their talents in the recitation of the *Gita*. In the case of the slightly older children, they are given a chance to discourse upon the *Gita*. This is a wonderful way to encourage children to study this sacred scripture.

5. In the evening, a special Satsang is held at which learned scholars, Yogis and Sannyasins discourse upon the holy scripture.

6. Leaflets, pamphlets and books containing the teachings of the *Gita*, as also translations of the holy scripture, are distributed.

Take a resolve on Gita Jayanthi that you will read at least one discourse of the *Gita* daily. Recite the Fifteenth Discourse before taking your meals. This is done at the Sivanandashram.

Keep a small pocket-sized edition of the *Gita* with you at all times. Mark a few verses in it which inspire you. Everyday, while you are waiting for your bus or train, or whenever you have a little leisure, pull out the book and read these verses. You will be ever inspired.

May you all lead the life taught by the *Gita*! May the *Gita*, the blessed Mother of the *Vedas*, guide and protect you! May it nourish you with the milk of the ancient wisdom of the *Upanishads*!

Glory to Lord Sri Krishna, the Divine Teacher! Glory to Sri Vyasa, the poet of poets, who composed the *Gita*! May his blessings be upon you all!

18

Hanuman Jayanthi

Yatra yatra raghunatha kirtanam;
Tatra tatra kritha masthakanjalim;
Bhaspavaari paripurna lochanam;
Maarutim namata raakshasanthakam.

MEANING: "We bow to Maruti, Sri Hanuman, who stands with his palms folded above his forehead, with a torrent of tears flowing down his eyes wherever the Names of Lord Rama are sung".

SRI HANUMAN is worshipped throughout India—either alone or together with Sri Rama. Every temple of Lord Rama has the *murti* or idol of Sri Hanuman. Hanuman is the Avatara of Lord Shiva. He was born of the Wind-God and Anjani Devi. His other names are Pavanasuta, Marutsuta, Pavankumar, Bajrangabali and Mahavira.

He is the living embodiment of Ram-Nam. He was an ideal selfless worker, a true Karma Yogi who worked desirelessly and dynamically. He was a great devotee and an exceptional Brahmachari or celibate. He served

LORD HANUMAN
Om Sri Hanumate Namah
87

Lord Rama with pure love and devotion without expecting any fruit in return. He lived to serve Rama. He was humble, brave and wise. He possessed all the divine virtues. He did what others could not do— crossing the ocean by uttering Ram-Nam, burning the city of Lanka, bringing the *sanjeevini* herb and restoring Lakshmana to life again. He brought both Sri Rama and Lakshmana from the nether world after killing Ahiravana.

He had devotion, power, knowledge, spirit of selfless service, power of celibacy and desirelessness. He never boasted of his bravery and intelligence.

He said to Ravana, "I am a humble messenger of Sri Rama. I have come here to serve Rama, to do His work. By the command of Lord Rama, I have come here. I am fearless by the Grace of Lord Rama. I am not afraid of death. I welcome it, if it comes while I am serving Lord Rama."

Mark here how humble Hanuman was! How very devoted he was to Lord Rama! He never said, "I am the brave Hanuman. I can do anything and everything."

Lord Rama Himself said to Sri Hanuman, "I am greatly indebted to you, O mighty hero! You did marvellous superhuman deeds. You did not want anything in return. Sugriva has his kingdom restored to him. Angada has been made the crown prince. Vibhishana has become king of Lanka. But you—you have not asked for anything at any time. You threw away the precious garland of pearls given to you by Sita. How can I repay your debts? I will always remain indebted to you. I give you the boon that you will live forever. All will honour and worship you like Myself. Your *murti* will be placed at the door of My temple and you will be worshipped and honoured first. Whenever My stories are recited or glories sung, your glory will be sung before Mine. You shall be able to do all that even I cannot do!"

Thus did Lord Rama praise Hanuman when the latter returned to Rama after finding out Sita in Lanka. Hanuman was not a bit elated. He fell down at the Lotus Feet of Lord Rama.

Lord Rama asked him, "O mighty hero! how did you cross the ocean?"

Hanuman humbly replied, "By the power and glory of Thy Name, my Lord!"

Again the Lord asked, "How did you burn Lanka? How did you save yourself?"

And Hanuman replied, "By Thy Grace, my Lord!"

What humility Sri Hanuman embodied!

There are many who want wealth in return for their services. Some do not want wealth, but they cannot resist name and fame. Others do not want any of these, but they want approbation or thanks. Still others want nothing, but they boast of their deeds. Hanuman was above all these. That is why he is recognised as an ideal Karma Yogi, an unsurpassed adept in Bhakti. His life is full of object lessons. Everyone should try his level best to follow the noble example of Hanuman.

His birthday falls on Chaitra Shukla Purnima (the March-April full moon day).

On this holy day, worship Sri Hanuman. Fast on this day. Read the *Hanuman Chalisa*. Spend the whole day in Japa of Ram-Nam. Sri Hanuman will be highly pleased and bless you with success in all undertakings.

Glory to Hanuman! Glory to His Lord, Sri Rama!

19

Krishna Janmashtami

THIS IS THE birthday of Lord Krishna, ths eighth Divine Incarnation. It falls on the 8th day of the dark half of the month of Bhadrapada (August-September). This is one of the greatest of all Hindu festivals. Lord Krishna was born at midnight. A twenty-four hour fast is observed on this day, which is broken at midnight.

Temples are decorated for the occasion. Kirtans are sung, bells are rung, the conch is blown, and Sanskrit hymns are recited in praise of Lord Krishna. At Mathura, the birthplace of Lord Krishna, special spiritual gatherings are organised at this time. Pilgrims from all over India attend these festive gatherings.

The Lord appeared when the moon entered the house of Vrishabha at the constellation of the star Rohini, on Wednesday, the 8th day of the second fortnight of the month of Sravana, which corresponds to the month of Bhadrapada Krishnapaksha according to the Barhaspatyamana, in the year of Visvavasu, 5,172 years ago (from 1945), which means 3227 B.C.

Study the *Bhagavatam* and the *Pancharatras*, which are equal to the *Upanishads*. You will know all about the glory of Lord Krishna, His Lilas and superhuman deeds. The eighth Avatara, Krishna, who has become the Beloved of India and the world at large, had a threefold objective: to destroy the wicked demons, to play the leading role in the great war fought on the battlefield of Kurukshetra (where he delivered His wonderful message of the *Gita*) and to become the centre of a marvellous development of the Bhakti schools of India.

There is no true science except devotion to Lord Krishna. That man is wealthy indeed who loves Radha and Krishna. There is no sorrow other than lack of devotion to Krishna. He is the foremost of the emancipated who loves Krishna. There is no right course, except the society of Sri Krishna's devotees. The Name, virtues and Lilas (divine pastimes) of Krishna are the chief things to be remembered. The Lotus Feet of Radha and Krishna are the chief objects of meditation.

Sri Krishna is the ocean of bliss. His soul-stirring Lilas, which are the wonder of wonders, are its waves. The honeyed music of His flute attracts the minds of His devotees from all three regions. His unequalled and unsurpassed wealth of beauty amazes the animate and the inanimate beings. He adorns His friends with His incomparable love.

His palms bear the signs of a lotus and discus, the right sole of His feet of a flag, lotus, thunderbolt, an iron goad, barley seed, and the Swastika. His left sole has the rainbow, triangle, water-pot, crescent, sky, fish, and a

LORD SRI KRISHNA
Om Namo Bhagavate Vasudevaya
93

cow's footprint. His Form is composed of condensed universal consciousness and bliss. His Body pervades the entire cosmos.

Devotion is the only means of attaining Lord Krishna. Bhakti kindles love for the Lord. When love is directed towards Krishna, man is freed from the bondage of the world.

Though Lord Krishna appeared in a human body, He had a divine body not composed of the five elements. He did not take any birth here in the usual sense of the term. He did not die. He appeared and disappeared through His Yoga Maya as He has declared in the *Gita*. This is a secret, known only to His devotees, Yogis and sages.

His enchanting form with flute in hand is worshipped in myriads of homes in India. It is a form to which is poured out devotion and supreme love from the hearts of countless devotees not only in India but also in the West. Millions of spiritual seekers worship Him and repeat His Mantra, *Om Namo Bhagavate Vasudevaya.*

Lord Krishna was great in knowledge, great in emotion, great in action, all at once. The scriptures have not recorded any life more full, more intense, more sublime and grander than the life of Sri Krishna.

Krishna has played various roles during His stay in the world. He was Arjuna's charioteer. He was an excellent statesman. He was a master musician; he gave lessons even to Narada in the art of playing the *veena*. The music of His flute thrilled the hearts of the Gopis and everyone else. He was a cowherd in Brindavan and

Gokul. He exhibited miraculous powers even as a child. He killed many demons. He revealed His Comic Form to His mother, Yasoda. He performed the Rasa Lila, the secret of which can only be understood by devotees like Narada, Gauranga, Radha and the Gopis. He taught the supreme Truth of Yoga, Bhakti and Vedanta to Arjuna and Uddhava. He had mastered every one of the sixty-four fine arts. For all these reasons He is regarded as a full and complete manifestation of God.

Incarnations of God appear for special reasons under special circumstances. Whenever there is much unrighteousness, whenever confusion and disorder set in on account of unrighteousness and baffle the well-ordered progress of mankind, whenever the balance of human society is upset by selfish, ruthless and cruel beings, whenever irreligion and unrighteousness prevail, whenever the foundations of social organisations are undermined, the great Incarnation of God appears in order to re-establish righteousness and to restore peace.

An Incarnation is the descent of God for the ascent of man. A ray from the Cosmic Being in His potential state of manifestation descends on earth with mighty powers to keep up the harmony of the universe. The work done by the Incarnation of God and His teachings produce a benign influence on human beings and help them in their upward divine unfoldment and Self-realisation.

The Incarnation comes to reveal the divine nature of man and makes him rise above the petty materialistic life of passion and egoism.

The greatest manifestations are called Incarnations proper. Rishis, Munis, prophets, sons of God and messengers of God are minor manifestations.

The Incarnations usually come with their particular or favourite groups or companions. Lord Rama came with Lakshmana, Bharata and Shatrughna. Lord Krishna came with Balarama, Devas and Rishis. Sanaka came with Sanandana, Sanatkumara and Sanatsujata. Some, like Sri Shankara and Ramanuja, come as teachers and spiritual leaders. Some, like Chaitanya, are born to instill devotion in the hearts of people and turn their minds towards God. The Incarnations proper, like Krishna, come only when there is widespread catastrophe in the world.

On the holy Krishna Janmashtami, the ladies in South India decorate their houses beautifully, ready to welcome the Lord. They prepare various sweetmeats and offer them to the Lord. Butter was Krishna's favourite, and this is also offered. From the doorway to the inner meditation room of the house the floor is marked with a child's footprints, using some flour mixed with water. This creates the feeling in them that the Lord's own Feet have made the mark. They treat the day as one of very great rejoicing. There is recitation of the *Bhagavatam*, singing and praying everywhere.

The Janmashtami is celebrated at the Sivananda Ashram, Rishikesh, with the following programme of intense spiritual activity:

1. During the preceding eight days, Japa of *Om Namo Bhagavate Vasudevaya* is done intensely.

96

2. Those who can, will recite the *Bhagavatam* during this period. Others will listen to it being recited.

3. On the birthday itself everyone fasts and spends the whole day in holy communion.

4. Everyone greets others with the holy Mantra, *Om Namo Bhagavate Vasudevaya.*

5. A grand *havan* is performed on that day.

6. There is continuous Satsang from 4a.m. early in the morning till night. Yogis, Sannyasins and learned men discourse upon the glorious life and teachings of the Lord.

7. From sunset people assemble in the elaborately decorated temple and sing the Lord's Names and glories.

8. Many hymns and portions of the *Bhagavatam*, especially the *Gopika Geetam*, are recited.

9. Towards midnight, there is a grand worship of Lord Krishna. The Lord is bathed with milk while His Name is chanted 108 times.

10. This worship concludes with offerings of flowers, waving of lights (Arati), and reading of that portion of the *Bhagavatam* which deals with the birth of Krishna. This synchronises with midnight, the hour of the Lord's birth, at which time the *murti* of the Lord is rocked in a beautifully decorated cradle. After this item, all the assembled devotees partake of the holy *prasad* or sacrament, and then retire, filled with the Grace and blessings of Lord Krishna.

If you cannot read the whole of the *Srimad Bhagavatam* during these days, at least you should recite the following four most important verses from the book. The leading two verses and the closing verse are the prologue and the epilogue respectively:

"Hear from Me the most secret knowledge coupled with the essential experience and its component parts.

"May you realise by My Grace, the knowledge of Myself and what form, qualities and actions I am endowed with.

1. "Before creation I alone existed. There was nothing, neither existence nor non-existence. I am that which remains after dissolution.

2. "Understand that to be Maya or illusion which is devoid of any purpose, which is not to be found in the Self and which is unreal like light and darkness.

3. "As the primary elements are amalgamated, with one another and also separate from one another at the same time, so I pervade the whole universe and am also separate from it.

4. "The aspirant should, by the method of positive and negative, know that thing which exists always and everywhere.

"Experience this truth through the highest superconscious state so that you will not be disturbed even by illusory objects".

There is another beautiful verse in the *Bhagavatam* which you can recite daily: "In days of yore, the Lord, born of Devaki, brought up in the house of Yasoda, killed the wicked Putana of illusive form and lifted the

Govardhana hill, killed Kamsa and the sons of the Kuru race, and protected the sons of Kunti. Thus is recited the essence of the ancient *Bhagavat Purana* consisting of the nectarine stories of the deeds of Lord Krishna".

May the blessings of Lord Krishna and Sri Radha be upon you all!

20

Shankara Jayanthi

Guru charanam, bhaja charanam,
  Satguru charanam, bhava haranam.
Maanasa bhajare, guru charanam,
  Dustara bhava saagara taranam.
Guru maharaaj guru jaya jaya,
  Para brahma satguru jaya jaya.

RELIGION IS realisation; it is not mere learning—this is the divine message which stands deeply in the minds of every Hindu. This is not a mere fancy. This is not a mental conception. This is not a stretch of imagination. It is not a coinage of the brain. Nor is it a decision arrived at by vehement vituperation and incongruent argumentation promulgated by an ordinary intellectual prodigy.

This is the assertion of Shankara, India's greatest philosopher-saint, the incarnation of Lord Shiva, reverently known as Srimath Adi Shankaracharya.

What can we take him for except the Lord Himself, who proclaims authoritatively and undauntedly: "I am the Self of all; I am the all; I am transcendent; I am one

BHAGAVAN SHANKARACHARYA
The Founder of the School of Monistic philosophy
Who is regarded as the Avatara of Lord Shiva.

without a second; I am the Absolute; I am the infinite Consciousness; I am homogeneous bliss".

Shankara is our Vedanta Guru. He was God incarnate. He was born at a time when Indian thought and culture were decaying; when they underwent sore distraction; when ethical glory and the widespread influence of the Buddhistic cult was gradually dying; when there was complete chaos and confusion; when innumerable sects sprang up and, with their own individual doctrines, confounded the masses; when evil social influences and blind superstitions, garbed falsely in the clothes of religion, attracted the credulous masses into a frenzy, and ambushed them into complete ignorance of the ultimate Reality. There were no less than seventy-two cults and sects of this type which carried away people from the right path.

The advent of Lord Krishna rejuvenated Hindu religion and saved many a soul from complete ruin, souls which would otherwise have subjugated themselves to passivism due to the misinterpretation of the *Vedas* and the *Upanishads*. In the same way, Shankara appeared on earth to deliver very many struggling souls. He set them free, and enlightened them through his peaceful, unostentatious persuasion and loving propaganda. Through his irresistible logic, he planted the triumphant banner of unique intellectual conquest over all other schools of philosophy. Before him, all other theories proved to be phantoms and fallacies.

It was only Shankara who gave the unshakable concrete form to Hinduism and established the unity and purity of enlightened Hindu thought and culture. Superstitions and corrupt practices melted away in no time.

The age-long six systems of theism which were suppressed by the prattlers re-emerged in their original glory only through the concerted efforts of Shankara.

His victory over other systems of philosophy was not due to a stubborn grip onto his own faith and reasoning without considering the pros and cons of others. He had mastered even the minutest intricasies of the other theories. The underlying currents of his thoughts were the foundations of the other systems. It is for this reason alone that his philosophy was recognised with much reverence by all the other schools of thought, despite differences in their superstructure.

The secret of his conquest and the charm therein lay in his most apt and reasonable illustrations in every case. He never based his arguments on theoretical axioms and untestified hypotheses, but entirely on integral experience. Further, all his arguments were based upon the *Vedas* as well, which are genuine and authoritative.

Shankara never entered into hot discussions to substantiate his case or disprove others' theories. With his gigantic intellect he poured out his masterly exposition in simple and clear terms with the same supreme authority of the *Gita, Upanishads* and the *Brahma Sutras*, the self-evident validity of the *Sruti Pramana*, and so on.

Above all, the philosophy of Shankara is not

restricted to the highly intellectual. It is within the easy reach of even the layman. With his profound knowledge, all-comprehensive learning, keen intuitive insight and convincing explanations, he has erected the strong edifice of Vedanta, equally accessible to the scholar and the layman. How effectively he prescribed "Bhaja Govindam" to the scholar who was racking his brains in committing various scriptures to memory!

Vedanta is not the only aspect of philosophy he has preached to the world. He has entered the heart of every earnest seeker after truth. He encourages the worship of various forms of the Lord and greatly advocates Bhakti. Without a tinge of partiality to one form or the other, he has composed innumerable hymns, each brimming with devotion and philosophical truth, each inculcating divine ecstasy and perennial joy even in the tender undeveloped mind. His untiring work for the welfare of mankind marks him out as a veritable, dynamic Karma Yogi, too.

At the background of all these, his devotion to his Guru is supermost. Mark what he says: "Any person who realises 'I am That Brahman' through the unparalleled mercy and glance of the Sadguru, loses all feelings of doubt and, with his mind free from illusion, attains liberation even while living in the body". How much efficacy and glory lie in devotion to the Guru!

Shankara Jayanthi falls on the 5th day of the bright half of Vaisakh (May-June). On this day, study his works, pray and meditate. May you be showered with his blessings!

21

Skanda Sashti

PROSTRATIONS and humble salutations to Lord Subramanya, the Supreme Being, who is the ruler of this universe, who is the indweller of our hearts, who is the second son of Lord Shiva, who is the beloved of Valli and Deivayanai, who bestows boons easily on His devotees, who is an embodiment of power, wisdom, love and bliss.

The mighty demon, Tarakasura, had been oppressing the celestials very much. He drove them out from heaven. All the gods then went to Brahma to appeal for help.

Brahma said to the gods: "O Devas! I cannot destroy Taraka, as he has obtained My grace through severe penances. But let Me give you a suggestion. Get the help of Cupid, the god of love. Induce him to tempt Lord Shiva who remains absorbed in His Yoga Samadhi. Let Lord Shiva unite with Parvati. A powerful son, Lord Subramanya, will be born to them. This son will destroy the demon that harasses you."

Indra, the chief of the gods, thereupon asked Cupid to go with his wife, Rati, and his companion Vasanta (the season of spring) to Mount Kailas, the abode of Shiva. Cupid carried out the instruction at once, for it was already springtime. Standing behind a tree, Cupid shot his arrow of passion towards Shiva whilst Parvati was placing some flowers in His hands. The moment their hands met, Shiva experienced a distracting feeling. He wondered what it was that disturbed His Yoga. He looked around and saw Cupid crouching behind the tree.

The Lord opened His "third eye", the inner eye of intuition, and Cupid was burnt to ashes by the fire that emanated from it. This is why the god of love is also called Ananga, which means "bodiless".

After burning Cupid, the Lord ascertained by His Yogic vision that the birth of Lord Subramanya was absolutely necessary to destroy the powerful Taraka. Shiva's seed was thrown into fire which, unable to retain it, threw it into the Ganges which in turn threw it into a reed forest. This is where Lord Subramanya was born; and hence he is called Saravanabhava—"born in a reed-forest". He became the leader of the celestial hosts and the destroyer of Taraka as Brahma had ordained.

Lord Subramanya is an incarnation of Lord Shiva. All incarnations are manifestations of the one Supreme Lord. Lord Subramanya and Lord Krishna are one.

Lord Krishna says in the *Gita*: "....of army generals, I am Skanda".

The Lord manifests Himself from time to time in various names and forms, for the sake of establishing righteousness and subduing the wicked.

Lord Subramanya is a ray born of the Consciousness of Lord Shiva. Valli and Deivayanai are His two wives. They represent the power of action and the power of knowledge respectively. He is the easily accessible Godhead in this dark age of ignorance and godlessness. In this He is no different from Hanuman. He bestows material and spiritual prosperity and success in every undertaking of His devotees, even if they show a little devotion to Him. He is worshipped much in South India. Some of His other names are Guha, Muruga, Kumaresa, Kartikeya, Shanmukha, Subramanya and Velayudhan.

In the picture, Lord Subramanya holds a spear in His hand, just as Lord Shiva holds the trident. This is an emblem of power. It indicates that He is the Ruler of the universe. His vehicle is the peacock. He rides on it. This signifies that He has conquered pride, egoism and vanity. There is a cobra under His feet which indicates that He is absolutely fearless, immortal and wise. Valli is on His one side, Deivayanai on the other. Sometimes He stands alone with His spear. In this pose He is known as Velayudhan; this is His Nirguna aspect which is free from the illusory power of Nature.

The six heads represent the six rays or attributes, namely, wisdom, dispassion, strength, fame, wealth and divine powers. They indicate that He is the source of the four *Vedas*, the Vedangas and the six schools of philosophy. They also indicate his control over the five organs of knowledge as well as the mind. They denote that He is the Supreme Being with thousands of heads and hands. That His head is turned in all directions signifies He is all-pervading. They indicate that He can multiply and assume forms at His will.

There are big temples of Lord Subramanya at Tiruchendur, in Udipi, Palani Hills, Ceylon and Tiruparankundrum. The Lord spent His childhood days in Tiruchendur and took Mahasamadhi at Kathirgamam. If anyone goes to Kathirgamam with faith, devotion and piety, and stays in the temple for two or three days, the Lord Himself grants His vision to the devotee. The devotee is filled with rich spiritual experiences. A big festival is held in the temple each year on Skanda Sashti. Thousands of people visit this place. "Mountains" of camphor are burnt on this occasion.

Skanda Sashti falls in November. It is the day on which Lord Subramanya defeated the demon, Taraka. Great festivals are held on this day with great pomp and grandeur. Devotees also do Bhajan and Kirtan on a grand scale. Thousands are fed sumptuously. Many incurable diseases are cured if one visits Palani and worships the Lord there. In South India, Lord Subramanya's Lilas are dramatized on stage.

In addition to the Skanda Sashti, devotees of Lord Subramanya observe weekly and monthly days in His honour. Every Friday, or the Kartigai Nakshatram day every month, or the 6th day of the bright fortnight,—all these are considered holy days by devotees. The 6th day of the month of Tulam (October-November) is the most auspicious of them all. This is the Skanda Sashti day.

In many places the festival commences six days prior to the Sashti itself and concludes on the day of the Sashti. During these days, people read and recite various hymns and stories connected with Lord Subramanya. They worship the Lord and take *Kavadi* (see below). They go on pilgrimages to the various Subramanya shrines.

The famous Nakkerar has composed the *Tirumuru-katrupadai* in His praise. He who studies this famous work daily, with devotion and faith, gets certain success in life, peace and prosperity. The *Tiruppugal* is another famous book in Tamil which contains the inspiring devotional songs of Arunagirinathar in praise of Lord Subramanya. The *Kavadichindu* songs are also in praise of the Lord. The *Skanda Sashti Kavacham* is another famous hymn in praise of Lord Subramanya, and is sung particularly on festive occasions.

The Kavadi Festival

Perhaps the most potent propitiatory rite that a devotee of Shanmukha undertakes to perform is what is known as the Kavadi. The benefits that the devotee gains from offering a Kavadi to the Lord are a millionfold greater than the little pain that he inflicts upon himself.

Generally, people take a vow to offer the Lord a Kavadi for the sake of tiding over a great calamity. Though this might on the face of it appear mercenary, a moment's reflection will reveal that it contains in it the seed for the supreme love for God. The worldly object is achieved, no doubt, and the devotee takes the Kavadi;

but after the ceremony he gets so God-intoxicated that his inner spiritual chamber is opened. This is also a method that ultimately leads to the supreme state of devotion.

Kavadi: The Kavadi varies in shape and size from the simple shape of a street hawker's storehouse (a wooden stick with two baskets at each end, slung across the shoulder) to the costly palanquin structure, profusely flower-bedecked and decoratively interwoven with peacock feathers. In all cases the Kavadi has a good many brass bells adorning it and announcing it as the Kavadi-bearer draws it along. As, very often, the Kavadi bearer observes silence, the bells are the only eloquent signs of a Kavadi procession.

Now, the two baskets hanging at either end of the Kavadi will contain rice, milk or other articles that the devotee has vowed to offer to Lord Subramanya. The more devout among them, and especially those who do it as a Sadhana, collect these articles by begging. They travel on foot from village to village, and beg from door to door. The villagers offer their articles directly into the basket of the Kavadi. The Kavadi-bearer continues begging until the baskets are full or the avowed quantity is reached, and then offers the Kavadi to the Lord. Some keen devotees undertake to walk barefooted from home to one of the shrines of Lord Subramanya, bearing the Kavadi all the way, and collecting materials for the offering. He has to walk a hundred miles sometimes! The people who place the articles in the baskets also receive the Lord's blessings.

The Kavadi-bearer: The Kavadi-bearer is required to observe various rules between the time he takes up the Kavadi and the day of the offering. He has to perform elaborate ceremonies at the time of assuming the Kavadi and at the time of offering it to the Lord. He also puts on the dress of a Pandaram, a Saivite mendicant. It consists of a saffron-coloured cloth, a scarlet conical cap, and a cane silver-capped at both ends. Lord Shiva, the Supreme Pandaram, Himself loves to wear this dress. The Pandaram lives on alms only. The Kavadi-bearer's bare chest is covered with several *rudraksha malas* (rosaries).

The Kavadi-bearer observes celibacy. He takes only pure, Sattwic food; he abstains from all sorts of intoxicating drinks and drugs. He continually thinks of God. Many of the Kavadi-bearers, especially those who do it as a spiritual Sadhana, impose various sorts of self-torture upon themselves. Some pass a sharp little spear through their tongue which is made to protrude out of the mouth. Others may pass a spear through the cheeks. This sort of piercing is done on other parts of the body also. The bearer does not shave; he grows a long beard. He eats only once a day. The spear pierced through his tongue or cheeks reminds him constantly of Lord Subramanya. It also prevents him from speaking. It gives him great power of endurance.

The Kavadi-bearer is in a high state of religious fervour. He dances in ecstasy. His very appearance is awe-inspiring; there is divine radiance on his face. Devotees often experience the state of feeling complete union with the Lord. Sometimes the Deity enters their body and possesses them for some time.

Agni Kavadi: This is the most difficult Kavadi-offering. With the Kavadi hanging on his shoulders, the devotee walks through a pit of burning coals. Hymns are sung in praise of the Lord by the devotees all around the pit. Drums are beaten. Incense is burnt. The entire atmosphere is awe-inspiring. The real devotee gets into a state of ecstasy and easily walks over the fire.

At the Sivananda Ashram, Rishikesh, Skanda Sashti is observed for six days, preceding and including the Sashti day.

1. Devotees of Lord Subramanya live on milk and fruit and do rigorous Sadhana.

2. All spiritual aspirants get up at 4a.m. during Brahmamuhurta and meditate on the Lord.

3. On each of the six days, all participants do as many *malas* of the Mantra *Om Saravanubhavaya Namah* as possible. They even greet one another with this Mantra.

4. Yogis and learned scholars deliver lectures on the Subramanya Tattwa or the divine sportings of the Lord. During the evening Satsang, hymns in praise of Lord Subramanya are sung. Readings are taken from my book *Lord Shanmukha and His Worship*. Devotees sing inspiring songs on the Lord.

5. Every day there is elaborate ceremonial worship of the image of Lord Subramanya installed in the Bhajan Hall.

6. On the last day, a grand *havan* (fire-worship) is

conducted. The Satsang is devoted entirely to the adoration of Lord Subramanya.

Pray from the bottom of your heart: "O Lord Subramanya! O all-merciful Lord! we have neither faith nor devotion. We do not know how to worship Thee in the proper manner, or to meditate on Thee. We are Thy children who have lost the way, forgotten the goal and Thy Name. Is it not Thy duty, O compassionate Father, to take us back? O Mother, will you not introduce us to Thy Lord? Mother's love for Her children is deeper and truer than any object in this world. Though we have become worthless and undutiful children, O beloved Mother Valli, pardon us! Make us dutiful and faithful. We are Thine from this very second. Always Thine. All is Thine. It is the Mother's duty to correct, educate, rectify and mould Her reckless children when they are straying aimlessly on the wrong path. Remove the gulf or the veil that separates us from Thee. Bless us. Enlighten us. Take us back to Thy Lotus Feet. We have nothing more to say. This is our fervent prayer to Thee and Thy Lord, our beloved and ancient Parents."

May Lord Subramanya shower His Grace upon you!

22

Ramnavmi

Om Sri Ram Jai Ram Jai Jai Ram

SALUTATIONS to Lord Rama, an Incarnation of Lord Vishnu, who is measureless, who is of the nature of pure Consciousness and bliss, who is the consort of Sita, Master of Sri Hanuman, and the Lord of the three worlds, who took His birth at His own will in order to establish righteousness, destroy the wicked and protect His devotees.

Ramnavmi or the birthday of Lord Rama falls on the 9th day of the bright fortnight of the month of Chaitra (March-April).

Rama was the Lord Hari Himself, incarnate on earth for the destruction of Ravana. He was well accomplished, beautiful and endowed with royal marks. His glory and prowess were unlimited. He was peerless on earth. He was free from malice. He was gentle. He was the protector of all His people. He always addressed them in gentle words. He never used any harsh words even when somebody provoked Him. He held sway over the whole world.

114

LORD SRI RAMA
Om Sri Ramaya Namah
115

Let Sri Rama be your ideal. Ideals are remembered and adored for the purpose of adopting them in your own life. The Ramnavmi celebration or the Vasanta Navaratri every year is an opportune period for us to saturate ourselves with the spirit of Lord Rama. We love and adore our ideals because we express thereby our yearning to unite with them. In our worship of God it is implied that we should be virtuous, good and perfect even as God is. Hence the wise instruction: "One should become divine in order to be able to worship God". One cannot be a real worshipper of Lord Rama unless one makes an honest attempt to grow in the virtues that the Lord represents. On the other hand, worship of Lord Rama is itself the surest means to develop such virtues.

One who approaches Sri Rama with love and worshipfulness becomes large-hearted, pure in spirit, good-natured and dispassionate in thought, word and deed. A true devotee of Lord Rama is His representative, with His power and His knowledge.

Lord Rama was the prince of the Ikshvaku race. He was virtuous and of manly strength. He was the Lord of the mind and the senses. Brave and valiant, He was yet gentle and modest. He was a sage in counsel, kind and sweet in speech, and most courteous and handsome in appearance. He was the master of all the divine weapons, and a great warrior. Ever devoted to the good and prosperity of His kingdom and His subjects, He was a defender of the weak and the protector of the righteous. Endowed with numerous wondrous powers of the mind, He was well versed in all sciences—in military science as well as the science of the Self.

Deep and unfathomed like the ocean, firm and steadfast like the Himalayan mountains, valiant like Lord Vishnu, He was the joy of Kaushalya. Though fierce like fire on the battlefield, He was calm like the cool breeze of the Mandara Hills, patient like Mother Earth, bounteous like the god of wealth and righteous like the lord of justice himself. In the pains and the griefs of His people, His heart swiftly sympathised with the sufferers. In the festive scenes which held them in joy, He like a father, shared their joys. By His honour and heroism, as well as by His gentleness and love for His subjects, He greatly endeared Himself to the hearts of His people. Such a great person was the Lord Rama!

Lord Rama was the best of men with a sterling character. He was the very image of love. He was an ideal son, an ideal brother, an ideal husband, an ideal friend and an ideal king. He can be taken to embody all the highest ideals of man. He led the ideal life of a householder to teach the tenets of righteousness to humanity. He ruled His people so well that it came to be known as Ram-Rajya, which meant the rule of righteousness, the rule which bestows happiness and prosperity on all.

The noblest lesson embodied in the *Ramayana* is the supreme importance of righteousness in the life of every human being. Righteousness is the spiritual spark of life. Cultivation of righteousness is the process of unfoldment of the latent divinity in man. The glorious incarnation of the Supreme Being in the form of Lord Rama has exemplified the path of righteousness. Let mankind follow His footsteps and practise the ideals cherished by Him, for it is only thus that there can be everlasting peace, prosperity and welfare in this world.

None but the righteous can be truly happy. None but he who has the correct sense of duty and the will for its implementation can be said to live worthily. One must be imbued with a definite conviction about the supremacy of moral principles, ethical values and spiritual ideals. These ought to guide one's day-to-day actions and serve as powerful means for the culture of the human personality. That is the purpose of life. That is the way to Self-realisation. That is the message and the mission of Lord Rama's life on earth.

To a devotee, Sri Rama is not simply a good and a great person, but God Himself. Rama was the son of King Dasaratha of Ayodhya, but He is also the divine omnipresent, omnipotent and omniscient God. The destruction of the ten-headed Ravana signifies the annihilation of the mind or the ten senses. Worship of Lord Rama is worship of the all-pervading Godhead Himself. Read the prayers offered by Mandothari and Brahma in the Yuddha Kanda of the *Ramayana*. They refer to Rama as the one Creator of the universe, the God of all, the Ruler of the universe.

Devotion to God is not a simple emotion. It is the result of intense dispassion and purity of heart and attitude. You should strive your utmost to possess the good qualities that are extolled in the *Ramayana* and exemplified in the life of Lord Rama. Otherwise, emotion may rise up in you temporarily to a kind of ecstasy, but you will not experience divine consciousness thereby. Devotion is a fruit which ripens gradually through the processes of self-restraint and virtue. Without intense dispassion there can be no real Sadhana for Self-realisation. Only after detachment from the world of things, is it possible to attain the Supreme Godhead. Remember this.

Devotion has absolutely nothing to do with age, caste, creed, position or sex. Generally, the worldly-minded people say: "We will practise meditation and devotion when we retire from service." This is a serious mistake. How can you do serious Sadhana after squeezing out all your energy in working? How will you be able to practise the strict Yogic discipline in your old age? Is there any certainty in life? No, the spiritual seeds of discipline and devotion must be sown in you while you are young, while your heart is tender and untainted. Then only will it strike a deep root, blossom forth and bear fruit when you become old and retire. Only then can you bravely face the god of death and meet him with a smile!

I shall tell you the means of attaining the final release from the great cycle of births and deaths. Devotion to Lord Rama is a great purifier of the heart. From devotion arises knowledge. From knowledge comes the realisation of the pure Self. Knowing this perfectly, one goes to the Supreme Abode and merges in the Supreme Self.

Without first developing devotion to Rama who is the Self, who lives in the hearts of all beings, who is all bliss and who is peerless, how can man cross the ocean of worldly life which has sorrow, pain and misery for its waves?

Do thou therefore worship Lord Rama who is Vishnu and the consort of Sita who is Lakshmi. Abandon all foolishness and enmity. Take to the service of Lord Rama.

The Lord is extremely fond of those who have surrendered themselves to Him. He has given this promise in the *Ramayana*: "To anyone who once takes shelter under Me and solicits 'I am Thine', I bestow fearlessness from all beings. This is My vow".

Even a great sinner who is full of evil qualities and who is fond of other people's wealth, is freed from all kinds of faults that pertain to worldly life if only he remembers the Lord always. He attains purity and goes to the supreme abode of the Lord.

The Name of Lord Rama is the greatest purifier of the heart. It wipes away all one's sins. Not only this, but it wipes away the sinful tendencies as well. The Name is sweeter than the sweetest of objects. It is the haven of peace. It is the very life of pure souls. It is the purifier of all purifying agencies. It quenches the consuming fire of worldly desires. It awakens the knowledge of God. It bathes the aspirant in the ocean of divine bliss. Glory to Sri Rama and His Name!

O Devotee! recite His Name, sing His glory and serve His Lotus Feet. Enthrone in your heart Lord Rama of dark hue, whose image is reflected in the heart of Lord Shiva. Blessed is the pious soul who uninterruptedly drinks the nectar of Sri Rama's Name which has been churned out of the ocean of the *Vedas*, which removes the impurities of the Kali Yuga or the iron age, which lives constantly on the lips of Lord Shiva, which is a sovereign remedy or unfailing specific to cure the disease of worldly existence and which is the life of Mother Sita.

Ram-Nam burns ignorance, passion and sin. With or without knowledge, correctly or incorrectly, when the word "Rama" is pronounced it showers a rain of good upon the devotee. Sri Rama is Brahman who takes one across the ocean of worldly existence. Rama is one in whom the Yogis sport, that is, the Self within.

Lord Shiva tells His consort Parvati: "This Ram-Nam is equal to the Lord's thousand Names, or repetition of the Mantra a thousand times".

I call this the anti-gossip tonic. When you find that you are wasting your time in gossip, repeat His Name several times. You can make up for the time lost, and the mind will be slowly weaned away from the habit of gossiping.

Sri Rama is also a wish-fulfilling tree. He will bestow upon you whatever you want! Just read what Lord Shiva further says:

"The seat of all good things, the destroyer of all impurities of this age of darkness, purer than purity itself, the food for the journey of aspirants on the path to salvation, their only resting place, the very life-breath of virtuous men, is the Divine Name of Sri Rama. So say the sages".

On the auspicious Ramnavmi day take a firm resolve that you will repeat Ram-Nam with every breath and that you will endeavour to lead a righteous life.

Ramnavmi is one of the most important festivals of the Vaishnava sect of the Hindus. However, even those who adore Lord Shiva celebrate the occasion. Some observe a strict fast on the day. Temples are decorated and the image of Lord Rama is richly adorned. The holy *Ramayana* is read in the temples. At Ayodhya, the birthplace of Sri Rama, a big fair is held on this day.

In South India the Sri Ramnavmi Utsavam is celebrated for nine days with great fervour and devotion. Those talented in the art of story-telling narrate the thrilling episodes of the *Ramayana*. The Kirtanists chant the holy Name of Rama and celebrate the wedding of Rama with Sita on this great day. It is an extremely colourful ceremony, highly inspiring and instructive, too.

At the Sivananda Ashram, Rishikesh, Ramnavmi is celebrated for nine days as follows:

1. Spiritual seekers do as much Japa as possible. The sacred Mantras *Om Sri Ramaya Namah* or *Om Sri Ram Jai Ram Jai Jai Ram* are chanted.

2. Devotees read the whole of the *Ramayana*, either the Sanskrit version of Sage Valmiki or the Hindi version of Saint Tulsidas, during these nine days.

Those who cannot recite the entire epic may read this single verse which contains in a nutshell the story of the

Ramayana: "Formerly, Sri Rama went to the forests, where Rishis did penance, and killed the illusive deer. Sita was carried away and Jatayu was killed. Rama met Sugriva, killed Vali and crossed the ocean. The city of Lanka was burnt by Hanuman. The demons, Ravana and Kumbhakarna, were then killed. Thus is recited the holy *Ramayana*".

3. Devotees greet one another with "Sri Ram" or "Jai Ram-ji-ki".

4. Those who have adopted Lord Rama as their favourite Deity observe a fast, taking only milk and fruit for all the nine days. Some fast only on the Ramnavmi day itself.

5. On the final or Ramnavmi day, there is a grand worship of Lord Rama in the gorgeously decorated temple. All the Vedic rituals including Laksharchana are performed.

6. A *havan* is also performed.

7. From four in the morning to late at night, there is Ram and Ram alone everywhere!

8. Leaflets, booklets and books relating to Lord Rama are distributed.

9. Special meetings are held in the evening at which discourses on the life and teachings of the Lord are delivered.

10. Earnest seekers take resolves to accelerate their spiritual progress.

O beloved seekers! time is fleeting. Know the value of time. Time is most precious. Utilise every second profitably. Do not procrastinate. Abandon all idle gossiping. Forget the past. Live every moment of your life for the realisation of the divine ideal and goal. Unfold your latent faculties. Grow, evolve and become a superhuman or a dynamic Yogi. Struggle hard and reach the goal of life.

May you all attain the final beatitude of life through intense devotion towards Lord Rama! May you live immersed in the ecstasy of divine love! May Sri Rama who is as effulgent as a million suns and who is adored by the gods and devotees, protect you all! May the blessings of Lord Rama be upon you all!

23

Pradosha Vrata

ALL THINGS in this vast creation function upon definite laws. There is always a beautiful system and sound rationale governing every phenomenon and process, mundane or mystical. Just as gross elements and physical forces operate variously under different sorts of states and conditions, so too the subtler and higher forces respond and react in the inner mystic planes and in the purely spiritual processes like worship, prayer, meditation, etc. Therefore, you will find definite injunctions for performing certain types of worship in the morning, certain other injunctions for the midday prayers and still others for the night worship. Again, some observances are meant to be done during certain phases of the moon, some when a particular star is in the ascendent, or at the time of a particular conjunction of planets.

The Pradosha worship is to be done in the evening twilight on the 13th day of each lunar fortnight. It is the worship of Lord Shiva for victory and success in all undertakings and the fulfilment of all your heart's cherished desires. When you wish to propitiate a superior person to obtain some favour from him, don't you naturally approach him at a moment when he is likely to be in a very pleasant frame of mind? You will perhaps see him after he has had a good dinner and is cheerfully chatting with a friend in a hearty, expansive mood. Even so, the Hindu, especially the Hindu who is engaged in the motivated type of worship usually selects the pleasant aspect of God for his worship. He performs it at a time which the ancient Rishis experienced as being the most efficacious in propitiating the Deity. The Pradosha worship is based on such mystic psychology.

Pradosha is the worship of Lord Shiva and Parvati in an extremely propitious mood. Repeatedly worsted in war by the demons, the gods approached Lord Shiva to bless them with a leader for their celestial hosts. They came at twilight on the 13th day of the lunar fortnight and found the Lord in the blissful company of His consort, Parvati. Hymned and glorified by them, Shiva immediately granted them their prayerful request. Hence the extreme auspiciousness of the period.

The *Skanda Purana* relates how Sandilya Muni prescribed this Vrata to a certain Brahmin lady. She came to the sage with two boys, her son Suchivrata and an orphan prince named Dharmagupta whose father was slain in battle and the kingdom overrun by enemies.

Acting upon the sage's advice, the woman and the boys performed the Vrata with great devotion. After four months, that is, during the eighth Pradosh, Suchivrata obtained the nectar pot and drank the ambrosia. The prince Dharmagupta won the hand of a celestial princess and, with the help of the celestial king himself, as ordered by Lord Shiva, his enemies were slain and his kingdom restored to him. Dharmagupta then attained the Lord's supreme abode. So easily, and yet so greatly is the Lord of Kailas pleased by this Vrata.

One who takes this Vrata fasts on that day, and keeps vigil at night after the fast is over. Bathing an hour before sunset the worshipper first performs a preliminary worship of Lord Shiva together with all the others of the divine family, namely, Parvati, Ganesha, Skanda and Nandi. After the Ganesha worship, Lord Shiva is invoked in the special *kalasha* placed on a square *mandala* with drawn lotus spread over with *darbha* grass. After the formal worship has been completed, the Pradosh story is read out and heard by the assembled devotees. This is followed by the recitation of the Maha Mrityunjaya Mantra 108 times. In the end the sacred *kalasha* water is taken, the sacred ash is applied to the forehead and the sacred water which was used to bathe the Lord is drunk. A gift of a pot, a cloth and an image of God is given to a Brahmin to conclude the worship.

A very important point to be remembered in this connection is that, during this auspicious period, all the hosts of celestial beings and gods come down from the heavens and attend the worship in their subtle forms. This adds immensely to the sanctity of the worship.

This Vrata is highly lauded by the scriptures and is of very great sanctity and importance to the worshippers of Lord Shiva. The mere sight of the Deity in a temple during this period will destroy all sins and bestow bountiful blessings upon the fortunate beholder. Even a single *bael* leaf (leaf taken from the wood-apple tree) offered to the Lord at this unique auspicious moment equals a hundred Mahapujas. It is usual to have special additional lights in the shrine during the Pradosha. To light even a single wick at this juncture is very meritorious and productive of untold benefits, material as well as spiritual. Most fortunate and blessed is the person who performs the Pradosha Vrata, for upon him Lord Shiva showers His choicest Grace and blessings in a very short time.

Here is the Yogic interpretation of the Pradosha Vrata:

According to the Shiva-Raja Yoga, concentration is directed towards the central point in the middle of the eye-brows where the spiritual light can be perceived by the Yogi who turns the vision inwards. The Yogi passes through various stages, all of which are sub-divisions of the four states, namely, waking, dreaming, deep sleep and the Fourth or superconscious state. Each one of these states is further sub-divided into four states, for example the waking-dreaming, waking-sleep, waking-Fourth and waking-waking. It will be seen that when the states are sub-divided in this manner, the first three states comprise a total of twelve sub-states. The thirteenth is the Fourth-waking. There is correspondence between this and the 13th day of the lunar fortnight, either bright or dark.

Those who worship Mother Shakti have certain beliefs of their own, one of which is that the Goddess that is worshipped acquires one ray on each of the days of the bright fortnight, starting from the first day. Thus on the full moon night, the Goddess would have received fifteen rays and would be fit for the final form of worship intended to benefit the worshipper in all ways. That is why the Navavarana worship is conducted on the full moon day.

The moon is believed to have a direct influence on the mind. Incidentally, the word *mati* means both the moon and the mind.

According to Shiva-Raja Yoga there are two channels through which the Prana flows. These are the Ida and the Pingala, ruled respectively by the moon and the sun. Midway between these two there is a third known as Sushumna. The Yogi is asked to start the practice of Yoga when the breath is passing through the lunar channel. This coincides with the flow of the breath through the left nostril. If, however, at the time of practice the flow is through the right nostril, the Yogi is asked to perform a special exercise by which to change the flow to the left. When the Yogi concentrates on the point between the eye-brows, he transcends, stage by stage the first twelve sub-states. The current of breath remains running through the lunar channel. The "moon" is gaining more and more strength. When the 13th day is reached, the spiritual power of the Yogi has correspondingly increased and he is in a condition to see the lights which appear in the nerve centre in between the eye-brows. In inverse proportion to the increase in concentration is the duration of the Yogi's breath. At the start of the practice, the breath will occupy a space of 16 fingers (inches approximately). The moment the concentration has led him from the waking to the dream state, the length of the breath becomes only 12 fingers. In this way when he reaches the 13th stage only 4 fingers of breath would remain. As this breath now circulates only within the nostril no breath is noticeable at the tip of the nose. From that moment the light is fixed permanently in the centre between the eye-brows, and the Yogi would have realised the object of his practice.

Let me now describe the actual process of Shiva-Raja Yoga:

The Yogi sits in utter darkness with the head and body erect, eyes open and the gaze directed to the centre of the eye-brows. He begins uttering the Mantra in his mind and, without restraining his breath, concentrates his gaze on the middle of the eye-brows, ever on the thought of the appearance of the lights which he expects at any moment. The resulting deep concentration yields the following fruit, in order.

First, he overcomes the distractions of his mind. He reaches a stage wherein he seems to hear somebody talking somewhere in the distance. The words are not distinct, but a sort of murmur is heard. Nevertheless, since his mind is elsewhere, he pays no attention to it. In fact, the sound comes from nowhere outside. It is his own mind that produces these sounds. The mind is actually functioning in its form as sound. Soon afterwards, this sound ceases, and he begins to see all sorts of visions, in the same manner as we see pictures in a movie. It appears, as if in a dream, that he is passing through hills of varying degrees of beauty, through seas and lakes of all sorts of colours and shapes, and through clouds of different hues. The clouds appear dark and thick at first and thin out gradually. These are scenes which are very pleasant to witness. But they are only thought-forms, an imagery created by the mind as it is functioning as a form. It is in this stage that the Yogi may hear musical notes as well, of the flute, violin, cymbals or any other instrument.

The Yogi then passes through an entirely different experience. He suddenly awakens from deep sleep. He does not remember when he got into the sleep state but he is conscious of the sudden awakening. (The truth is that he had not slept at all. His mind became a complete blank, he lost consciousness of the workings of the mind, which was nonetheless still active all the time. When he regained consciousness, he suddenly felt his awareness once again.) He is tempted to examine himself to see if his posture is still erect and if his eyes are still fixed between his eye-brows. Finding no change in these he realises that the temporary loss of consciousness was only a stage which he passed through in his Yoga.

Next comes the stage when he feels as if something of the nature of a hot nail is pricking him at the centre of his eye-brows. In the earlier period of his practice there will merely be this sensation. But as he advances, this is followed by the appearance of the lights. Even then there are various stages which have to be passed before the lights get their proper shape.

At first a yellow and a red light appear, the red being in the centre and two yellow flame-like lights on either side. After a few days, all these colours pass away and he begins to see a steady light of the shape and colour of the moon. As days advance this grows brighter and brighter and the whole room in which the Yogi sits is illumined gradually, starting at the intensity of twilight until it becomes a flood of bright light. Yet, in this state nothing that is in the room is seen; other things (which are not there!) begin to appear. They come and go with amazing rapidity, and reveal many things to him.

Thus far, we have dwelt upon only the first four stages of the entire series of sixteen stages which have to be passed through by the Shiva-Raja Yogi before he finally attains union with Lord Shiva. The details of the experiences in each stage vary from man to man as also from day to day. But, in the main, these are the stages:

At first, one is aware of what transpires about him. He is in the waking part of the waking stage. Then the pictures come in the dream part of his waking state. The feeling of overpowering sleep occurs in the deep sleep part of the waking state. The appearance of the light occurs in the Fourth part of the waking stage.

Likewise, the dream and the deep sleep states also have their four sub-divisions which have to be passed. When the Yogi comes to the thirteenth stage, he is in the waking part of the Fourth state. The real vision of Lord Shiva in the form of Self-Consciousness now begins.

The Form of Lord Shiva appears before him as though coming out of the lights which began in stage four of the sixteen stages. From this stage onwards the mind loses its sense of separate activity. It becomes absorbed in the Self within.

On the 13th lunar day Nature assists the worshipper in waking up from his mental deep sleep and in becoming aware of the Fourth state. The Yogi who practises his Yoga on the Pradosha day gets these experiences of Lord Shiva quite readily.

Similar to the above is the significance of worshipping Lord Ganesha on the 4th day of the lunar fortnight. This corresponds to the Fourth part of the waking state, when the lights are first seen. On the 8th day or the Ashtami, Mother Durga is adored—this corresponds to the Fourth part of the dream state. Ekadashi or the 11th day corresponds to the deep sleep part of the deep sleep state. In this state there is complete unawareness of the mind. This is the most favourable moment for a direct contact with God, the Indweller. If we fast and pray on that day, we can reduce our bodily activities to the minimum and can have the vision of the Lord who resides in our heart.

If we thus analyse the rationale of our holy days, we discover that our ancients took particular care to effect a synthesis of Yoga—Karma, Jnana and Bhakti.

At the Sivananda Ashram, Rishikesh, a special *havan* and an elaborate worship are conducted for the health and long life, success and prosperity of all. The Lord's sacred *prasad* is sent to devotees all over the world.

24

Satya Narayana Vrata

YOU ARE all familiar with Narada Rishi. He is the Triloka Sanchari—the one who moves about in the three worlds. When he once visited the earth plane, there was great misery. He was unable to find a way to relieve human suffering. He at once approached Lord Narayana and related to Him the sad state of affairs on earth.

Lord Narayana said to Narada, "O venerable Rishi, let people observe the Satya Narayana Vrata in the evening of Shankranti or Purnima. Let them all hear the story (Katha) of Satya Narayana. All miseries will come to an end. There is no doubt of this."

Rishi Narada thereupon returned to earth and preached the glory of the Satya Narayana Vrata. Many observed the vow without taking any food during the course of the day and attained what they desired. All were happy and prosperous.

The observance of the Satya Narayana Vrata does not cost much. You need only give a small gift to the pundit who comes to read the story and then distribute some *prasad* which also need not be very costly. Some wheat flour and sugar will make up the *prasad*. A little curd and some fruit are required. Even the poorest man can observe this Vrata.

In North India the vow is observed by the vast majority of people. It takes about three hours to complete the whole observance. It is generally observed on the full moon day, particularly the Kartik, Vaisakh, Sravan and Chaitra Purnimas and the Shankranti day. It can also be done on new moon days.

Five stories are connected with this Vrata. They speak about the glory of Lord Narayana and His Grace, His *prasad*, and of the incalculable benefit derived by observing the Vrata. He who hears these stories with faith, devotion and one-pointedness of mind derives considerable benefit. The first of these is the story of Narada, narrated above. The other stories have great moral lessons in them concerning truthfulness, fulfilment of promises, etc.

2. The Story of a Poor Brahmin

There was a very poor Brahmin. He was living on alms. Lord Narayana appeared before him in the form of an old Brahmin, asked him to observe the Satya Narayana Vrata and gave him His word of assurance that he would be free from poverty, by observing this Vrata. The Brahmin acted accordingly. All his desires were fulfilled.

3. The Story of a Wood-cutter

The same Brahmin then did the Vrata on a grand

scale. A poor wood-cutter entered the compound of the Brahmin to drink some water. The Katha of Satya Narayana was going on. The wood-cutter, attracted only by the skill of the story-teller, sat down and heard it with rapt attention. He also was inspired to observe the Vrata in his house. He took some *prasad* and ate it.

Then he went to the market-place and sold his bundle of fuel. He received double the usual amount for his fuel. He immediately purchased the things that were necessary for the Vrata and observed it along with his family members, with intense faith and devotion. All his desires were fulfilled. He enjoyed everything that was possible on this earth plane. After death he attained the supreme abode of Satya Loka where Truth alone prevails.

4. The Story of a Merchant

Once upon a time King Ulkamukha reigned over the earth. He was a devotee of Lord Satya Narayana. The queen, too, was very pious. One day they observed a fast and performed the Satya Narayana Vrata on the banks of the holy Bhadrasheela.

A merchant named Sadhu came to the king and asked him what he was doing. The king explained to the merchant all about the Satya Narayana Vrata. When Sadhu returned home he narrated to his wife, Lilavathi, the glory of the Satya Narayana Vrata as he heard it from the king. Thereupon, both resolved to observe it, provided they were blessed with a child. Lilavathi soon brought forth a girl whom they named Kalavathi.

Sadhu now thought that he would postpone the Vrata till after his daughter was married. The wedding of Kalavathi took place in course of time, but Sadhu had entirely forgotten his resolve. After some time he went to foreign countries for trade along with his son-in-law.

Lord Narayana felt it was high time He reminded Sadhu of his resolve. One night, while Sadhu was at a place called Ratnasarpur, he was suddenly arrested and imprisoned along with his party by the royal police. The police suspected them to be thieves. At the same time, thieves had robbed the property of Sadhu in his native place.

Meanwhile, poor Lilavathi and Kalavathi were leading a miserable life in the streets. One day Kalavathi went to get alms and it so happened that she received some *prasad* of Lord Satya Narayana from a temple. She came back to her mother and pleaded that they, too, should observe the Vrata. They thus observed the Vrata and worshipped Lord Satya Narayana.

That very day, the king of Ratnasarpur dreamt that Sadhu and his party were not really guilty of any theft and that they should be released else he would be destroyed along with his relatives. The king at once released Sadhu and his party from prison, giving them double the value for their merchandise.

Sadhu was on his way back to his native village when Lord Satya Narayana appeared before him in the guise of a mendicant and asked him what he had in the boat. Sadhu suspected that the mendicant might ask him for some money. He therefore replied that there were bundles of leaves only in the boat.

The mendicant replied, "Your words will come true, O merchant!"

That night, while Sadhu was on his usual round of checking the contents of the boat, he found that the jewels had indeed all turned into leaves! He realised that this was due to uttering falsehood to the mendicant. He quickly went out in search of the mendicant, found him in a secluded spot and begged his pardon.

The mendicant sternly said, "You have not kept up your promise of observing the Satya Narayana Vrata." Then he revealed his true identity to the merchant, gave him words of solace and disappeared.

Sadhu came back to his boat and found that all the bags contained jewels again. He worshipped Lord Satya Narayana with intense faith and devotion.

After five days, Sadhu reached his native place. He sent a message to inform his wife and daughter of his arrival. At the time when the messenger arrived to give the news, Lilavathi and Kalavathi were hearing the Satya Narayana Katha. When they had finished the worship they went to meet Sadhu, but, alas! they had forgotten to take the *prasad* of the Lord.

Lord Satya Narayana wanted to point out their carelessness in not taking the *prasad*. The boat with its wealth and their son-in-law sank. The son-in-law struggled in desperation for his life. Sadhu who was on the shore prayed and worshipped the Lord. A divine voice was heard in the sky: "Kalavathi has not taken

My *prasad*. So this has happened." Kalavathi hurried back to her house and ate the *prasad*. She returned, and with sheer joy on her face, beheld both her father and her husband who was miraculously saved through the Grace of Lord Satya Narayana. Even the boat and the jewels were recovered miraculously. All rejoiced. Sadhu narrated all that had happened during his travel and how he was saved by the Lord when in distress.

Thenceforth, the couple, Sadhu and Lilavathi, regularly observed the Satya Narayana Vrata during Purnima and Shankranti, and lived happily ever after. They attained the blissful abode of Lord Narayana.

5. The Story of King Tungadhwaja

One day King Tungadhwaja went out hunting. After walking a long distance he was overcome by fatigue. He sat under a banyan tree. Some boys of the cowherd class were performing the Vrata of Satya Narayana in the vicinity of the banyan tree. The boys came to know that a king was resting under the tree. One of them respectfully took some *prasad* and placed it before the king.

The king did not want to attend the function, nor prostrate before the Lord. He did not take the *prasad* either. In fact, he cast a look of disgust at the offering, and proudly returned to his capital.

The Lord wanted to teach the king a lesson. The king was given the news that his sons and daughters died and his whole property was destroyed. He inwardly understood that this was due to the disrespect he had shown to the Lord and His *prasad*. He repented very much for his wrong doing.

With a sore but repentant heart, he made his way to the banyan tree where the boys had worshipped the Lord. He himself now performed the worship with intense faith and devotion. Lord Satya Narayana showered His Grace upon the king. He got back his lost property and his children. The king thereafter regularly worshipped the Lord and lived happily.

He who observes this Vrata, which is even being observed by the gods themselves, with faith, devotion and self-surrender; he who hears the sacred story of Lord Satya Narayana with faith and devotion; he who attends the worship and eats the *prasad*—he certainly attains health, wealth and joy. He is uplifted from the mire of worldliness and the clutches of death. He finally abides in the Truth.

In the Kali Yuga, worship of Lord Hari through the Satya Narayana Vrata makes one happy, peaceful and prosperous. This is the truth described in the ancient epics.

25

Shivaratri

THIS FALLS on the 13th (or 14th) day of the dark half of Phalgun (February-March). The name means "the night of Shiva". The ceremonies take place chiefly at night. This is a festival observed in honour of Lord Shiva. Shiva was married to Parvati on this day.

People observe a strict fast on this day. Some devotees do not even take a drop of water. They keep vigil all night. The Shiva Lingam is worshipped throughout the night by washing it every three hours with milk, curd, honey, rose water, etc., whilst the chanting of the Mantra *Om Namah Shivaya* continues. Offerings of *bael* leaves are made to the Lingam. *Bael* leaves are very sacred as, it is said, Lakshmi resides in them.

Hymns in praise of Lord Shiva, such as the *Shiva Mahimna Stotra* of Pushpadanta or Ravana's *Shiva Tandava Stotra* are sung with great fervour and devotion. People repeat the Panchakshara Mantra, *Om Namah Shivaya*. He who utters the Names of Shiva during Shivaratri, with perfect devotion and concentration, is freed from all sins. He reaches the abode of

Shiva and lives there happily. He is liberated from the wheel of births and deaths. Many pilgrims flock to the places where there are Shiva temples.

The Story of King Chitrabhanu

In the Shanti Parva of the *Mahabharata*, Bhishma, whilst resting on the bed of arrows and discoursing on Dharma, refers to the observance of Maha Shivaratri by King Chitrabhanu. The story goes as follows.

Once upon a time King Chitrabhanu of the Ikshvaku dynasty, who ruled over the whole of Jambudvipa, was observing a fast with his wife, it being the day of Maha Shivaratri. The sage Ashtavakra came on a visit to the court of the king.

The sage asked, "O king! why are you observing a fast today?"

King Chitrabhanu explained why. He had the gift of remembering the incidents of his previous birth.

The king said to the sage: "In my past birth I was a hunter in Varanasi. My name was Suswara. My livelihood was to kill and sell birds and animals. One day I was roaming the forests in search of animals. I was overtaken by the darkness of night. Unable to return home, I climbed a tree for shelter. It happened to be a *bael* tree. I had shot a deer that day but I had no time to take it home. I bundled it up and tied it to a branch on the tree. As I was tormented by hunger and thirst, I kept awake throughout the night. I shed profuse tears when I thought of my poor wife and children who were starving and anxiously awaiting my return. To pass

LORD SHIVA
Om Namah Shivaya
143

away the time that night I engaged myself in plucking the *bael* leaves and dropping them down onto the ground.

"The day dawned. I returned home and sold the deer. I bought some food for myself and for my family. I was about to break my fast when a stranger came to me, begging for food. I served him first and then took my food.

"At the time of death, I saw two messengers of Lord Shiva. They were sent down to conduct my soul to the abode of Lord Shiva. I learnt then for the first time of the great merit I had earned by the unconscious worship of Lord Shiva during the night of Shivaratri. They told me that there was a Lingam at the bottom of the tree. The leaves I dropped fell on the Lingam. My tears which I had shed out of pure sorrow for my family fell onto the Lingam and washed it. And I had fasted all day and all night. Thus did I unconsciously worship the Lord.

"I lived in the abode of the Lord and enjoyed divine bliss for long ages. I am now reborn as Chitrabhanu."

Spiritual Significance of the Ritual

The scriptures record the following dialogue between Sastri and Atmanathan, giving the inner meaning of the above story.

Sastri: It is an allegory. The wild animals that the hunter fought with are lust, anger, greed, infatuation, jealousy and hatred. The jungle is the fourfold mind, consisting of the subconscious mind, the intellect, the ego and the conscious mind. It is in the mind that these "wild animals" roam about freely. They must be killed. Our hunter was pursuing them because he was a Yogi. If you want to be a real Yogi you have to conquer these evil tendencies. Do you remember the name of the hunter in the story?

Atmanathan: Yes, he was called Suswara.

Sastri: That's right. It means "melodious". The hunter had a pleasant melodious voice. If a person practices Yama and Niyama and is ever conquering his evil tendencies, he will develop certain external marks of a Yogi. The first marks are lightness of the body, health, steadiness, clearness of countenance and a pleasant voice. This stage has been spoken of in detail in the *Swetaswatara Upanishad.* The hunter or the Yogi had for many years practised Yoga and had reached the first stage. So he is given the name Suswara. Do you remember where he was born?

Atmanathan: Yes, his birthplace is Varanasi.

Sastri: Now, the Yogis call the Ajna Chakra by the name Varanasi. This is the point midway between the eyebrows. It is regarded as the meeting place of the three nerve currents (Nadis), namely, the Ida, Pingala and the Sushumna. An aspirant is instructed to concentrate on that point. That helps him to conquer his desires and evil qualities like anger and so on. It is there that he gets a vision of the Divine Light within.

Atmanathan: Very interesting! But how do you explain his climbing up the *bael* tree and all the other details of the worship?

145

Sastri: Have you ever seen a *bael* leaf?

Atmanathan: It has three leaves on one stalk.

Sastri: True. The tree represents the spinal column. The leaves are threefold. They represent the Ida, Pingala and Sushumna Nadis, which are the regions for the activity of the moon, the sun and fire respectively, or which may be thought of as the three eyes of Shiva. The climbing of the tree is meant to represent the ascension of the Kundalini Shakti, the serpentine power, from the lowest nerve centre called the Muladhara to the Ajna Chakra. That is the work of the Yogi.

Atmanathan: Yes, I have heard of the Kundalini and the various psychic centres in the body. Please go on further; I am very interested to know more.

Sastri: Good. The Yogi was in the waking state when he began his meditation. He bundled up the birds and the animals he had slain and, tying them on a branch of the tree, he rested there. That means he had fully conquered his thoughts and rendered them inactive. He had gone through the steps of Yama, Niyama, Pratyahara, etc. On the tree he was practising concentration and meditation. When he felt sleepy, it means that he was about to lose consciousness and go into deep sleep. So he determined to keep awake.

Atmanathan: That is now clear to me; you certainly do explain it very well. But why did he weep for his wife and children?

Sastri: His wife and children are none other than the world. One who seeks the Grace of God must become an embodiment of love. He must have an all-embracing

146

sympathy. His shedding of tears is symbolical of his universal love. In Yoga also, one cannot have illumination without Divine Grace. Without practising universal love, one cannot win that Grace. One must perceive one's own Self everywhere. The preliminary stage is to identify one's own mind with the minds of all created beings. That is fellow-feeling or sympathy. Then one must rise above the limitations of the mind and merge it in the Self. That happens only in the stage of Samadhi, not earlier.

Atmanathan: Why did he pluck and drop the *bael* leaves?

Sastri: That is mentioned in the story only to show that he had no extraneous thoughts. He was not even conscious of what he was doing. All his activity was confined to the three Nadis. The leaves, I have said before, represent the three Nadis. He was in fact in the second state, namely, the dream state, before he passed into the deep sleep state.

Atmanathan: He kept vigil the whole night, it is said.

Sastri: Yes, that means that he passed through the deep sleep state successfully. The dawning of day symbolises the entrance into the Fourth state called Turiya or superconsciousness.

Atmanathan: It is said that he came down and saw the Lingam. What does that mean?

Sastri: That means that in the Turiya state he saw the Shiva Lingam or the mark of Shiva in the form of the inner lights. In other words, he had the vision of the Lord. That was an indication to him that he would realise the supreme, eternal abode of Lord Shiva in course of time.

Atmanathan: So it appears from what you say that the sight of the lights is not the final stage?

Sastri: Oh no! That is only one step, albeit a difficult one. Now think of how the story continues. He goes home and feeds a stranger. A stranger is one whom you have not seen before. The stranger is no other than the hunter himself, transformed into a new person.

The food was the likes and dislikes which he had killed the previous night. But he did not consume the whole of it. A little still remained. That was why he had to be reborn as King Chitrabhanu. Going to the world of Shiva (Salokya) is not enough to prevent this. There are other stages besides Salokya. These are Samipya, Sarupya and finally Sayujya. Have you not heard of Jaya and Vijaya returning from Vaikunta?

Atmanathan: Yes, I have understood now.

Lord Shiva's Assurance

When creation had been completed, Shiva and Parvati went out to live on the top of Mount Kailas. Parvati asked, "O venerable Lord! which of the many rituals observed in Thy honour doth please Thee most?"

The Lord replied, "The 14th night of the new moon, in the dark fortnight during the month of Phalgun, is my most favourite day. It is known as Shivaratri. My devotees give me greater happiness by mere fasting than by ceremonial baths and offerings of flowers, sweets and incense.

"The devotee observes strict spiritual discipline in the day and worships Me in four different forms during each of the four successive three-hour periods of the night. The offering of a few *bael* leaves is more precious to Me than the precious jewels and flowers. My devotee should bathe Me in milk at the first period, in curd at the second, in clarified butter at the third, and in honey at the fourth and last. Next morning, he should feed the Brahmins first and, after performing the prescribed ceremonies, he can break his fast. O Parvati! there is no ritual which can compare with this simple routine in sanctity."

Parvati was deeply impressed by the speech of Lord Shiva. She repeated it to Her friends who in their turn passed it on to the ruling princes on earth. Thus was the sanctity of Shivaratri broadcast all over the world.

The two great natural forces that afflict man are Rajas (the quality of passionate activity) and Tamas (that of inertia). The Shivaratri Vrata aims at the perfect control of these two. The entire day is spent at the Feet of the Lord. Continuous worship of the Lord necessitates the devotee's constant presence in the place of worship. Motion is controlled. Evils like lust, anger, and jealousy, born of Rajas are ignored and subdued. The devotee observes vigil throughout the night and thus conquers Tamas also. Constant vigilance is imposed on the mind. Every three hours a round of worship of the Shiva Lingam is conducted. Shivaratri is a perfect Vrata.

The formal worship consists of bathing the Lord.

149

Lord Shiva is considered to be the Form of Light (which the Shiva Lingam represents). He is burning with the fire of austerity. He is therefore best propitiated with cool bathing. While bathing the Lingam the devotee prays: "O Lord! I will bathe Thee with water, milk, etc. Do Thou kindly bathe me with the milk of wisdom. Do Thou kindly wash me of all my sins, so that the fire of worldliness which is scorching me may be put out once for all, so that I may be one with Thee—the One alone without a second."

At the Sivananda Ashram, Rishikesh, the Shivaratri festival is celebrated in the following manner.

1. All spiritual aspirants fast the whole day, many of them without taking even a single drop of water.

2. A grand *havan* is performed for the peace and welfare of all.

3. The whole day is spent in doing the Japa of *Om Namah Shivaya* and in meditation upon the Lord.

4. At night all assemble in the temple and chant *Om Namah Shivaya* the whole night.

5. During the four quarters of the night the Shiva Lingam is worshipped with intense devotion.

6. Sannyas Diksha is also given on this day to sincere seekers on the path.

Offer this inner worship to Lord Shiva daily: "I worship the jewel of my Self, the Shiva residing in the Lotus of my heart. I bathe Him with the water of my pure mind brought from the river of faith and devotion. I worship Him with the fragrant flowers of Samadhi—all this so that I may not be born again in this world."

Shivaratri

Here is another formula for the supreme worship of the Lord: "O Shiva! you are my Self. My mind is Parvati. My Pranas are your servants. My body is your house. My actions in this world are your worship. My sleep is Samadhi. My walk is circumambulation of you. My speech is your prayer. Thus do I offer all that I am to you."

26

Vaikunta Ekadashi

VAIKUNTA Ekadashi falls in the month of Marga-seersha (December-January). This is observed with all solemnity in the temples of Lord Vishnu. Fasting is prescribed on all Ekadashis, that is, the 11th day of the lunar fortnight, twice a month.

In this Kali Yuga, even if just one Ekadashi is observed with dispassion, faith and devotion, and if the mind is wholly fixed on Hari, one is freed from the rounds of birth and death. There is no doubt about this. The scriptures give us their assurance on this point.

Devotees fast on this day, observe vigil the whole night and do Japa, Hari Kirtan and meditation. Some do not take even a drop of water. Those who are unable to fast completely can take some light fruit and milk.

No rice should be taken on Ekadashi days. This is very important. The sweat that fell down from the head of Brahma assumed the form of a demon and said to the Lord, "O Lord! now give me an abode to dwell."

Brahma replied, "O demon! go and dwell in the rice particles eaten by men on Ekadashi day and become worms in their stomach."

For this reason rice is prohibited on Ekadashi. If one observes the Ekadashi fast regularly, Lord Hari is propitiated. All sins are destroyed. The mind is purified. Devotion gradually develops. Love for God becomes intense. Orthodox people in South India observe complete fasting and vigil even on ordinary Ekadashi days. For the devotees of Lord Vishnu, every Ekadashi is a very sacred day.

Benefits of Fasting

Nowadays, many educated people do not observe fasting on this sacred day. This is due to the impact of the dark, vicious, materialistic forces. When the intellect develops a little, people begin to enter into arguments and unneccesary discussions. Intellect is a hindrance on the spiritual path. They who have not developed the heart but who have developed their intellect begin to doubt and question at every step. They are led astray. They want a "why" and a "how" for everything. They want "scientific" explanations for all phenomena.

God is beyond proofs and presumptions. One has to approach religion and the scriptures with great faith, reverence and purity of heart. Then only are the secrets of religion revealed unto him like the apple in the palm of one's hand. Does anybody ask his mother to prove who is his father?

Fasting controls passion. It checks the emotions. It controls the senses also. It is a great penance. It purifies the mind and the heart. It destroys a multitude of sins. Fasting controls the tongue in particular which is the deadliest enemy of man. Fasting overhauls the respiratory, circulatory, digestive and urinary systems. It destroys all the impurities of the body and all sorts of poisons. It eliminates uric acid deposits. Just as impure gold is rendered pure by melting it in the crucible again and again, so also this impure mind is rendered purer by repeated fasting.

Young and robust Brahmacharis (celibates) should observe fasting whenever passion troubles them. Only then will they have very good meditation, as the mind will be rendered calm. The chief object of fasting is to render the system calm so that one is able to practise meditation rigorously during that period.

Withdraw the senses and fix the mind on God. Pray to God to guide you and to throw a flood of light on your spiritual path. Say with feeling: "O God, guide me! Protect me, protect me! I am Thine, I am Thine! Forsake me not!" You will be blessed with purity, light and strength. Follow this Sadhana on the days that you fast, Ekadashi days in particular.

Fasting is one of the ten canons of Yoga. However, avoid excessive fasting. It will produce weakness. Use your common sense. If you cannot fast for the full twenty-four hours, at least fast for 10-12 hours and then take some milk and fruit. Gradually increase your fast to 15 hours and then up to 24 hours. Fasting makes a man strong, both spiritually and mentally.

In his code, the *Manu Smriti*, the great Hindu lawgiver, Manu, prescribes fasting for the removal of the five capital sins. Diseases that are pronounced incurable by doctors are cured by fasting. Occasionally, a complete fast is greatly desirable for all to keep up good health, to give adequate rest to the internal organs and maintain celibacy. All diseases have their origin in overeating and verily fasting is the only method to cure this.

Complete fasting helps to control sleep. Taking recourse to tea to control sleep is not desirable. You will not gain any spiritual strength if you depend on an external agent. During fasting avoid all company. Live alone. Utilise your time in Sadhana. When breaking a fast do not take a heavy meal or a heavy food that is hard to digest. Milk or some fruit juice is beneficial.

Moderation in eating and withdrawal of the senses in Yogic meditation are the obverse and the reverse of the same coin. Moderation consists in taking a little food or water just to keep the body in good working order.

In the *Gita* you will find: "Verily, Yoga is not for him who eats too much, nor who abstains to excess, nor who sleeps too much, nor to the excessively wakeful".

The Yogi withdraws his senses from the particular sense objects. The senses are made to turn into or get involved into the mind. When one is fully established in these two practices, supreme control of the senses is achieved.

Once there was a demon, Mura, who oppressed the gods. The gods approached Lord Hari for protection. Hari sent Yoga Maya to kill the demon. Yoga Maya carried out the behests of the Lord successfully.

Then the Lord said to Yoga Maya, "Those who

observe Ekadashi will be freed from all sins, and you will be called by the name Ekadashi."

King Ambarisha was a great votary of Lord Hari. He practised the Ekadashi Vrata for a year. Ambarisha obtained His Grace. On one occasion he fasted for three consecutive days. He was about to break the fast when Rishi Durvasa appeared as his guest. The king received him with due respect and requested him to take his meals. The Rishi agreed and went to bathe in the river. The king waited patiently for a long time, but the Rishi did not return. Time was running out; if the king did not eat anything before the day ended his Vrata would not bear fruit. And if he ate, he would be showing disregard to the Rishi. As a compromise the king took a little water to serve both the conditions.

When Durvasa returned from his bath, he knew exactly what had happened, and was angry. He tore a hair from his tuft and charged it to kill Ambarisha. The king was unmoved. The discus of Lord Vishnu destroyed the power of the hair of Durvasa. It now followed the Rishi wherever he went and tried to destroy him.

Rishi Durvasa went to Brahma and Shiva for help, but to no avail. He went to Lord Hari who said to him, "I am dependent on My devotees. My heart is in the possession of My devotees. Go thou, therefore, to Ambarisha; beg his pardon and thou shalt be saved."

Ambarisha thereupon prayed to the charged hair to desist from its course, and saved the Rishi. Durvasa thanked him from the bottom of his heart.

27

Vara Lakshmi Vrata

LORD SHIVA describes the glory of this Vrata in the *Skanda Purana*. It is performed by a woman whose husband is still living. Maha Lakshmi is the abode of all auspiciousness and prosperity. This worship of Maha Lakshmi is done to obtain good progeny, and for the health and long life of the husband.

The Vrata is observed on the Friday immediately preceding the full moon day of the month of Sravan (August-September). After a purificatory bath, the lady should put on a clean, fresh cloth and make a *mandala* with the drawing of a lotus upon it. A *kalasha* filled with rice and topped with fresh mango leaves, a coconut and cloth are placed on the *mandala* and Lakshmi is invoked therein. Fresh grains are used in the worship as they convey the idea of growth and prosperity.

After the worship of the *kalasha*, follows the worship of Ganesha, then the worship of the *raksha* or the sacred thread. Now the main worship of Vara Lakshmi begins and the *raksha* is worshipped a second time. It is then tied to the right hand of the lady. After the worship various auspicious articles are given as charity to some

deserving lady whose husband is alive. This lady is also
fed with dainties.

Lakshmi not only bestows wealth and all sorts of
material prosperity, but also imparts divine wisdom to
all Her devotees. She is Vidya Shakti. She introduces
Her devotees to Her Lord. She recommends them to
Her Lord for their salvation.

She is the power of Lord Narayana who is also
known as Lord Vishnu or Lord Hari. Narayana is
God's aspect of preservation. He is an embodiment of
Shuddha Sattwa. Lakshmi is His causal body. She is
Maya, the illusory power of Nature. She deludes the
whole world by Her veiling power and projects it
through Her projecting power. She Herself as Vidya-
Lakshmi enlightens the spiritual aspirant. Beauty,
grace, a picturesque scenery or charming landscape,
modesty, love, prosperity, music, the five elements and
their combinations, the internal organs, mind, Prana,
intellect—all these are Her manifestations.

Without Lakshmi even Sannyasins cannot do propaganda or preaching work or run their institutions. They
are in fact more in need of Lakshmi than the householders because they have to do great dynamic work for
humanweal. Sri Shankara worshipped Devi, Lakshmi
and Saraswathi for success in his work. All great
prophets and divine messengers who have done great
spiritual work in the past were devotees of Mother
Lakshmi, Devi and Saraswathi.

May Goddess Lakshmi bless you all! Let us repeat
Her Mantra:

MOTHER LAKSHMI
The Giver of Prosperity and Happiness
Om mahaadevyai cha vidmahe;
Vishnu patnyai cha dheemahi
Tanno lakshmi prachodayat.

159

28

Special Observances

THE ECLIPSE

WHEN THE gods and the demons churned the milky ocean in days of yore, nectar came out of it. Lord Vishnu assumed the form of Mohini, a charming lady, deluded the demons and distributed the nectar only among the gods. But Rahu had disguised himself as a god. The sun and the moon pointed this out to Mohini who immediately slashed off the demon's head. Since the nectar had by then already reached up to the neck, he did not die. Thus the head came to be known as Rahu and the body as Ketu. To avenge this betrayal, Rahu and Ketu periodically eclipse the sun and the moon.

Astronomically speaking, when the sun, the moon and the earth are all in line, with the moon or the earth at the centre, a solar or lunar eclipse takes place respectively.

At the time of the eclipse, people bathe in the sacred rivers. They do charitable acts. They give cows, money and gold. The day after the eclipse they feed the poor, the Brahmins and the Sadhus. After the eclipse they clean their houses, vessels, etc., and take a bath before they start cooking.

One should not take food during the eclipse. When the eclipse begins the food should by then have been digested. One should take food only after seeing the sun or the moon free from the eclipse. When the clear sun or the moon is not seen before sunset or sunrise, in the case of the solar and lunar eclipse respectively, food can be taken only after the sun or the moon is seen the next day.

Pregnant women should not see the sun or the moon during the time of the eclipse. If they do the child born may have some kind of defect. He may be born deaf, dumb or blind. Householders are forbidden from sexual intercourse on the day of the eclipse, for the same reason.

At this time one should take great care in avoiding bleeding, scorpion stings, etc. These have disastrous results. Even an earthworm has a poisonous effect when it bites one during an eclipse.

Those who do Japa at the time of the eclipse derive great benefits. The effect of Japa and Sankirtan during the eclipse contributes towards relieving the suffering of humanity and also of the planets. These people receive the blessings of the gods. They attain perfection quickly. Those who wish to tap the subtle force locked in the Mantra that will cure scorpion stings should stand in water and repeat the appropriate Mantra.

The little intellect cannot understand many things in this universe. Hence, have faith in the words of sages.

Ignorance has eclipsed Self-knowledge. However, this eclipse will disappear. You will shine in your own glory. This is the spiritual significance of the eclipse.

MAHALAYA AMAVASYA

The dark fortnight of Aswayuja (September-October) is known as the Mahalaya Paksha or the fortnight specially sacred for offering oblations to the departed ancestors. The last day of this period, the new moon day, is considered as the most important day in the year for performing obsequies and rites.

The renowned hero of the *Mahabharata*, Karna, when he left the mortal coil, ascended to the higher worlds and the great charity he had done here was returned to him hundredfold. But, it was all gold and silver; there was no food, as he had not done any food-charity! He prayed to the god of death. So, he was sent back to earth for fourteen days, to make up for this deficiency.

For fourteen days, he fed Brahmins and the poor, and offered oblations of water. On his return to the higher regions, he had food in plenty. It is these fourteen days that are commemorated in the Mahalaya Paksha. Due to the grace of the god of death, it has been ordained that offerings made during this period benefit all the departed souls, whether they are connected to you or not.

Charity in the form of food is important during this observance. Life depends upon food. You cannot preach religion to empty stomachs. This human body is the most important vehicle for realising God. How precious must food be which keeps the body fit for Yoga! The gift of food is the greatest gift. Therefore, give food in plenty, not only during the Mahalaya fortnight but all through the year.

Om Tat Sat Brahmaparnamastu

Philosophy of Idol Worship

THE IDOL is a support for the neophyte. It is a prop in his spiritual childhood. A form or image is necessary for worship in the beginning. It is an external symbol of God for worship. It is a reminder of God. The material image calls up the mental idea. Steadiness of mind is obtained by image worship. The worshipper will have to associate the ideas of infinity, omnipotence, omniscience, purity, perfection, freedom, holiness, truth and omnipresence with the form of worship he chooses.

It is not possible for all to fix the mind on the Absolute. A concrete form is necessary for the vast majority for practising concentration. To behold God everywhere and to practise the presence of God is not possible for the ordinary man. Idol worship is the easiest form of worship for the modern man.

A symbol is absolutely indispensable for fixing the mind. The mind wants a prop to lean upon. It cannot hold a conception of the Absolute in the initial stages. Without the help of some external aid the mind cannot be centralised. In the beginning, therefore, concentration or meditation is not possible without a symbol.

Everyone an Idol Worshipper

Idol worship is not peculiar to Hinduism. Christians worship the Cross. They have the image of the Cross in their mind. The Muslims keep the image of the Kaaba stone when they kneel and do prayers. The people of the whole world, save a few Yogis and Vedantins, are all worshippers of idols. They keep some image or the other in their mind.

The mental image also is a form of idol. The difference is not one of kind, but only of degree. All worshippers, however intellectual they may be, generate a form in the mind and make the mind dwell on that image.

Everyone is thus an idol worshipper. Pictures, drawings, etc., are only forms of idols. A gross mind needs a concrete symbol as a prop and a subtle mind requires an abstract symbol. Even a Vedantin has the symbol Om to fix his wandering mind. It is not only the pictures or images in stone and in wood that are idols, but dialectics and great leaders also become idols. So, why condemn idolatry?

A Medium for Establishing Communion With God

Idols are not the idle fancies of sculptors, but are shining channels through which the heart of the devotee is attracted to God and flows towards Him. Though apparently the image is worshipped, the devotee feels the presence of the Lord in it and pours out his devotion unto it. It is the appalling ignorance of the modern sensual man that clouds his vision and prevents him from seeing Divinity in the lovely and enchanting idols of His forms.

The wonderful scientific advances of this century ought to convince one of the glory of idol worship. How are the songsters and orators confined to a small box-like thing called a radio or a T.V.? The latter are merely lifeless, mechanical structures which would break into a thousand pieces if thrown violently; and yet, if you know how to handle it, you can hear through it the music and see through it the pictures occurring several thousands of miles away. Even as you catch the sound-waves of people all over the globe through the radio and T.V., it is possible to commune with the all-pervading Lord through the medium of an idol. The divinity of the all-pervading God is vibrant in every atom of creation. There is not a speck of space where He is not. Why do you then say that He is not in the idols?

There are many who would glibly say: "Oh, God is an all-pervading formless Being. How can He be confined to this idol!" Are these people ever conscious of His omnipresence? Do they always see Him and Him alone in everything? No. It is their ego that prevents them from bowing to the idols of God and with that motive they put this lame excuse forward.

Empty vessels make much sound. A practical man who does meditation and worship, who is full of knowledge and real devotion, always keeps silent. He influences and teaches others through silence. He alone knows whether an idol is necessary in the beginning of concentration or not.

However intellectual one may be, one cannot concentrate without the help of some symbol. An intellectual or a learned person may say on account of his pride and vanity: "I do not like an idol. I do not wish to concentrate on a form." He cannot concentrate on the formless One. He thinks that people will laugh at him when they come to know that he is meditating on an idol. He never does any meditation on the formless One. He simply talks and argues and poses. He wastes his life in unnecessary discussions only. An ounce of practice is better than tons of theories.

Intellect is a hindrance in the vast majority of intellectual persons. They say that the existence of Brahman is guess-work, the superconscious state is a bluff and Self-realisation is an imagination of the Vedantins. Deluded souls! They are steeped in ignorance. They are carried away by their secular knowledge which is mere husk when compared to the knowledge of the Self. There is no hope of salvation for such people. First, their wrong impressions should be flushed by good impressions through Satsang. Then only will they realise their mistakes. May the Lord bestow on them clear understanding and thirsting for real knowledge!

A Symbol of God

The idol is a substitute or symbol. The image in a temple, though it be made of stone, wood or metal, is precious for a devotee as it bears the mark of his Lord, as it represents something which he holds holy and eternal. A flag is only a small piece of painted cloth, but to a soldier it stands for something that he holds very dear. He is prepared to give up his life in defending his flag. Similarly, the image is very dear to a devotee. It speaks to him in its own language of devotion. Just as the flag arouses martial valour in the soldier, so also the image arouses devotion in the devotee. The Lord is superimposed on the image and the image generates divine thoughts in the worshipper.

A piece of ordinary white paper or coloured paper has no value. You throw it away. But, if there is the stamp of the Government on the paper (currency note), you keep it safe in your money pocket or trunk. Even so, an ordinary piece of stone has no value for you. You throw it away. But, if you behold the stone idol of Lord Krishna at Pandharpur or any other idol in shrines, you bow your head with folded palms, because there is the stamp of the Beloved Lord on the stone. The devotee superimposes on the stone idol his own Lord and all His attributes.

When you worship an image, you do not say: "This image has come from Jaipur. It was bought by Prabhu Singh. Its weight is 50 lbs. It is made of white marble. It has cost me Rs.500." No! You superimpose all the attributes of the Lord on the image and pray: "O Inner Ruler! You are all-pervading. You are omnipotent, omniscient and all-merciful. You are the source of everything. You are eternal, unchanging. You are the life of my life, the Soul of my soul! Give me light and knowledge! Let me dwell in Thee for ever!"

When your devotion and meditation become intense

and deep, you do not see the stone image. You behold the Lord only who is pure Consciousness. Image worship is very necessary for beginners.

An Integral Part of the Cosmos

For a beginner, the idol is an absolute necessity. By worshipping the idol, the Lord is pleased. The idol is made up of the five elements. The five elements constitute the body of the Lord. The idol remains an idol, but the worship goes to the Lord.

If you shake hands with a man, he is highly pleased. You have touched only a small part of his body and yet he is happy. He smiles and welcomes you. Even so, the Lord is highly pleased when a small portion of His cosmic body is worshipped. An idol is a part of the body of the Lord. The whole world is His body. The devotion goes to the Lord.

The worshipper superimposes on the image the Lord and all His attributes. He does the sixteen forms of reverence to the Lord. First, the Presence of the Deity is invoked. Then a seat is offered, the feet are washed, water is offered, and then hospitality is offered. The idol is bathed, dressed and invested with the sacred thread. Sandal paste is applied to its forehead, flowers are offered, and incense is burnt. Then a lamp is lit and waved before the Deity. Food is now offered, together with the burning of camphor. A gift of gold is offered. Finally (the sixteenth step), the Deity is bidden farewell.

In these external forms of worship, the inner love finds expression. The wandering mind is fixed now in

169

this form of worship. The aspirant gradually feels the nearness of the Lord. He attains purity of heart and slowly annihilates his egoism.

To the worshipper who has faith in the symbol, any kind of image is the body of the Lord, be it made of stone, clay, or brass, or be it a picture, drawing, etc. Such worship can never be idolatry. All matter is a manifestation of God. God is present in everything. Everything is an object of worship, for all is a manifestation of God who is therein worshipped. The very act of worship implies that the object of worship is superior and conscious. This way of looking at things must be attained by the devotee. The untutored mind must be trained to view things in the above manner.

Idol worship Develops Devotion
Idol worship makes concentration for man simple and easy. You can bring before your mind's eye the great pastimes of the Lord in His particular incarnation in which you view Him. This is one of the easiest modes of Self-realisation. It is one that suits the majority of people today.

Just as the picture of a famous warrior evokes heroism in your heart, so also a look at the picture of God will elevate your mind to divine heights. Just as the child develops the maternal feeling by caressing, nursing and protecting its doll made of rags, and suckles it in an imaginary manner, so also the devotee develops the feeling of devotion by worshipping the idol and concentrating on it.

Unveiling the Divinity in the Idol

Regular worship and other modes of demonstrating our inner feeling of recognition of divinity in the idol unveil the Divinity latent in it. This is truly a wonder and a miracle. The picture comes to life. The idol speaks. It will answer your questions and solve your problems. The God in you has the power to awaken the latent Divinity in the idol. It is like a powerful lens that focusses the sun's rays onto a bundle of cotton. The lens is not fire and the cotton is not fire either, nor can the sun's rays by themselves burn the cotton. However, when all three are brought together in a particular manner, fire is generated and the cotton is burnt. Similar is the case with the idol, the aspirant, and the all-pervading Divinity. The idol is the lens which brings into focus the all-pervading rays of Divinity and lights up the aspirant with divine illumination.

God is enshrined in the idol. From here, He will protect you in a special manner. The idol will perform miracles. The place where it is installed is at once transformed into a temple, nay, a Vaikunta or Kailas in reality. Those who live in such a place are freed from miseries, from diseases, from failures and from worldliness itself. The awakened Divinity in the idol acts as a guardian angel blessing all, conferring the highest good on those who bow to it.

The Image—A Mass of Consciousness

The idol is only a symbol of the Divine. A devotee does not behold therein a block of stone or a mass of metal. It is an emblem of God for him. He visualises the indwelling Presence in the idol. All the sixty-three Nayanar saints of South India attained God-realisation through worship of the Shiva Linga, the image of Lord Shiva. For a devotee, the image is a mass of consciousness. He draws inspiration from it. It guides him. It talks to him. It assumes the human form to help him in a variety of ways.

The image of Lord Shiva in the temple at Madura in South India helped the fuel-cutter and the old woman. The image in the temple at Tirupati assumed a human form and gave witness in the court to help His devotees. These are marvels and mysteries. Only the devotees understand them.

When Idols Become Alive

For a devotee or a sage, there is no such thing as insentient matter. Everything is consciousness. The devotee actually beholds the Lord in the idol. Narsi Mehta was put to the test by a king. The king said, "O Narsi! if you are a true, sincere devotee of Lord Krishna, if, as you say, the idol is Lord Krishna Himself, let this idol move." According to the prayer of Narsi Mehta, the idol did move. The sacred bull, Nandi, standing before Shiva's idol, took the food offered by Tulsidas. The idol of Krishna played with Mirabai. It was full of life and consciousness for her.

When Appayya Dikshita went to the Tirupati temple in South India, the Vaishnavas refused to grant him admission. The next morning they found that the idol of

Lord Vishnu in the temple had changed to the idol of Lord Shiva. The priest was greatly astonished and startled. He asked pardon and prayed to Appayya Dikshita to change the idol again to that of Lord Vishnu.

Kanaka Das was a great devotee of Lord Krishna in Udipi, in the district of South Kanara, in South India. He was not allowed to enter the temple on account of his low birth. Kanaka Das went round the temple and saw a small window at the back of the temple. He seated himself in front of the window. He was soon lost in singing songs in praise of Lord Krishna. Many people gathered round him. They were very powerfully attracted by the sweet melody of his music and the depth of his devotion. Lord Krishna turned round to enable Kanaka Das to get His Darshan. The priests were struck with wonder. Even today, pilgrims are shown the window and the place where Kanaka Das sat and sang.

The idol is the same as the Lord, for it is the vehicle of the expression of the Mantra-consciousness which is the Deity. The devotee should regard the idol in the temple with the same attitude of respect and reverence that he would evince should the Lord Himself appear before him in person and speak to him in articulate sound.

Vedanta and Idol Worship

A pseudo-Vedantin feels ashamed to bow before an idol in the temple. He feels that his Advaita (attitude of oneness) will evaporate if he prostrates himself. Study

the lives of the reputed Tamil saints—Appar, Sundarar, Sambandhar, and others. They all had the highest Advaitic realisation. They saw Lord Shiva everywhere. Yet, they visited all temples of Shiva, prostrated before the idol and sang hymns which are on record till today. The sixty-three Nayanar saints solely practised the worship of the idols of Shiva and attained God-consciousness thereby. They swept the floor of the temple, collected flowers, made garlands for the Lord and put lights in the temple. They were illiterate, but attained the highest realisation. They were practical Yogis and their hearts were saturated with pure devotion. They were embodiments of Karma Yoga. All practised the Yoga of synthesis. The idol was all consciousness to them, not a mere block of stone.

Madhusudana Swami, who had Advaitic realisation, who beheld oneness of the Self and who had the feeling of oneness with all creation, was intensely attached to the form of Lord Krishna with flute in His hands.

Tulsidas realised the all-pervading essence. He had Cosmic Consciousness. He communed with the all-pervading, formless Lord. And yet, his passion for Lord Rama with bow in His hand did not vanish. When he was at Brindavan, beholding the idol of Lord Krishna with flute in hand, he said, "I will not bow my head to this form." At once Lord Krishna's form assumed the form of Lord Rama. Then only he bowed his head.

Tukaram also had the same cosmic experience as that of Tulsidas. He sings in one of his songs: "I see my Lord all-pervading, just as sweetness pervades the sugar-

cane", and yet, he always speaks of his Lord Vittala of
Pandharpur with His hands on the hips. Mirabai also
realised her identity with the all-pervading Krishna,
and yet she was not tired of repeating again and again,
"My Giridhar Nagar!"

From the above facts, we can clearly infer that one
can realise God through worship of the idol; that the
idol is a great aid for the realisation of the Lord in His
all-pervading, formless aspect also; that the worship of
the idol is very essential for the purpose of concentration and meditation in the beginning; and that such a
worship is not in any way a hindrance to the attainment
of God-realisation.

Those who vehemently attack idol worship are
groping in extreme darkness and ignorance, and have
no real knowledge of worship. They enter into
unnecessary, vain debates and discussions against idol
worship to show that they are learned persons. They
have not done any real Sadhana at all. They are persons
who have made idle talking and tall talk their habit and
profession. They have ruined themselves. They have
unsettled the minds of countless persons and ruined
them also. The whole world worships idols alone in
some form or another.

The mind is disciplined in the beginning by fixing it
on a concrete object or symbol. When it is rendered
steady and subtle, it can be fixed on an abstract idea
such as Aham Brahma Asmi. As one advances in
meditation, the form melts in the formless and one
becomes absorbed in the formless essence. The worship

of idols is, therefore, not contrary to the view of Vedanta. It is rather an aid to the highest Vedantic realisation.

Conclusion

Idol worship is only the beginning of religion. Certainly it is not its end. The same Hindu scriptures which prescribe idol worship for beginners, also speak of meditation on the Infinite or the Absolute and contemplation on the significance of *Tat Twam Asi* for advanced aspirants.

There are different grades of worship. The supreme state is Self-realisation. Second in rank is meditation on the Supreme Self. The third is the worship of symbols. The fourth is the performance of rituals and pilgrimages to holy places. The *Shastras*, the Gurus, are like kind mothers. They take hold of the hands of the aspirants and take them step by step till they are established in the highest superconscious state. Glory to the Hindu Rishis who take aspirants from the lower to the higher form of worship!

Beloved children of the Lord! Shed your ignorant disbelief this moment. Enshrine supreme, unshakable, living faith in your heart this very moment. Recall to your mind the glorious examples of saints of the past. They believed, and they reaped the rich spiritual harvests. You too can enjoy great peace, happiness and prosperity here, and attain Him here and now if you have faith in idol worship.